On Core
Mathematics

Middle School Grade 7

HOUGHTON MIFFLIN HARCOURT

Table of Contents Grade 7

COMMON CORE

Unit 4   Geometry: Modeling Geometric Figures

Unit 5   Geometry: Circumference, Area, and Volume

Unit 6   Statistics and Probability: Populations and Sampling

Unit 7   Probability and Simulations

Learning the Common Core State Standards

Has your state adopted the Common Core standards? If so, then you'll be learning both mathematical content standards and the mathematical practice standards that underlie them. The supplementary material found in *On Core Mathematics Grade 7* will help you succeed with both.

Here are some of the special features you'll find in *On Core Mathematics Grade 7*.

INTERACTIVE LESSONS

You actively participate in every aspect of a lesson. You carry out an activity in an Explore and complete the solution of an Example. This interactivity promotes a deeper understanding of the mathematics.

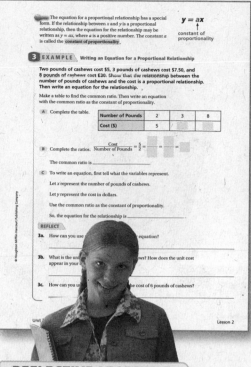

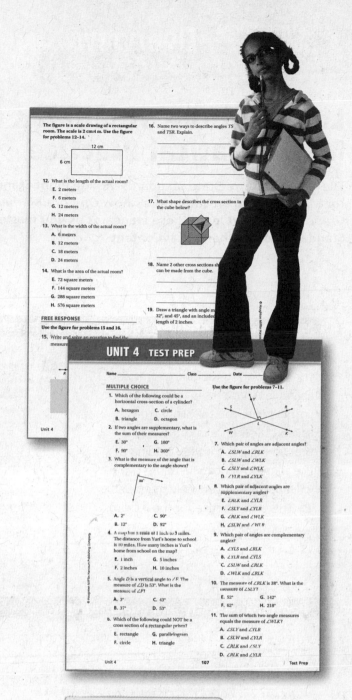

REFLECTIVE LEARNING

You learn to be a reflective thinker through the follow-up questions after each Explore and Example in a lesson. The Reflect questions challenge you to really think about the mathematics you have just encountered and to share your understanding with the class.

TEST PREP

At the end of a unit, you have an opportunity to practice the material in multiple choice and free response formats common on standardized tests.

PROBLEM SOLVING CONNECTIONS

Special features that focus on problem solving occur near the ends of units. They help you pull together the mathematical concepts and skills taught in a unit and apply them to real-world situations.

Learning the Standards for Mathematical Practice

The Common Core State Standards include eight Standards for Mathematical Practice. Here's how *On Core Mathematics Grade 7* helps you learn those standards as you master the Standards for Mathematical Content.

① Make sense of problems and persevere in solving them.

In *On Core Mathematics Grade 7*, you will work through Explores and Examples that present a solution pathway for you to follow. You are asked questions along the way so that you gain an understanding of the solution process, and then you will apply what you've learned in the Try This and Practice for the lesson.

> **1 EXPLORE** Calculating Markups
>
> To make a profit, a store manager must mark up the prices on the items he sells. A sports store buys skateboards from a supplier for *s* dollars. The store's manager decides to mark up the price for retail sale by 42%.
>
> A The markup is _____% of the price, *s*.
>
> B Find the amount of the markup. Use a bar model.
>
> 0.42s   1s
>
> The white bar represents the cost of the skateboard, _____.
>
> The grey section is _____% of _____. This can be written as a decimal, _____.
>
> C Add _____ to the cost of the skateboard to find the retail price.
>
> Retail price = ☐ + ☐
>
> Original cost   Markup
>
> D You can combine like terms in the expression

② Reason abstractly and quantitatively.

When you solve a real-world problem in *On Core Mathematics Grade 7*, you will learn to represent the situation symbolically by translating the problem into a mathematical expression or equation. You will use these mathematical models to solve the problem and then state your answer in terms of the problem context. You will reflect on the solution process in order to check your answer for reasonableness and to draw conclusions.

> **REFLECT**
>
> 1a. How can you tell that the final depth for Tomas will be deeper than −20 feet without doing any calculations?
>
> **TRY THIS!**
>
> 2e. Why do you evaluate the power in the equation before multiplying?

③ Construct viable arguments and critique the reasoning of others.

Throughout *On Core Mathematics Grade 7*, you will be asked to make conjectures, construct a mathematical argument, explain your reasoning, and justify your conclusions. Reflect questions offer opportunities for cooperative learning and class discussion. You will have additional opportunities to critique reasoning in Error Analysis problems.

REFLECT

1c. Conjecture Work with other students to make a conjecture about the sign of the sum when the addends have the same sign.

12. Error Analysis Kate says the radius of the circle is 8 feet. What is Kate's error? Find the correct diameter of the circle.

C = 25.12 ft
x ft

1. Combine your results with your classmates and calculate the experimental probability. Do you think this value is a better approximation of the theoretical probability than your result from only 10 trials?

④ Model with mathematics.

On Core Mathematics Grade 7 presents problems in a variety of contexts such as science, business, and everyday life. You will use mathematical models such as expressions, equations, tables, and graphs to represent the information in the problem and to solve the problem. Then you will interpret your results in the problem context.

1 EXPLORE Finding Total Cost

CC.7.RP.3

The bill at a restaurant for the Smith family came to $40. They want to leave a 15% tip. What is the total cost of the meal?

A Find the amount of the tip. Use a bar model

Total Cost

$40

Tip = 15%

The white bar represents $40. It is divided into ____ equal pieces.

Each section represents ____ %, or $ ____.

The tip is 15% or ____ sections of the model.

1 section = $ ____, so $\frac{1}{2}$ of a section = $ ____.

$1\frac{1}{2}$ sections = $ ____ + $ ____ = $ ____.

The tip is $ ____.

B Find the total cost of the meal.

To find the total cost of the meal, add together the bill total and the tip.

	+	=
Bill total	Tip	Total Cost

C Another way to find the tip is to multiply the bill total by the percent of the tip.

Write 15% as a decimal. ____

	×	=
Bill total	Percent	Tip

	+	=
Bill total	Tip	Total Cost

5 Use appropriate tools strategically.

You will use a variety of tools in *On Core Mathematics Grade 7*, including manipulatives, paper and pencil, and technology. You might use manipulatives to develop concepts, paper and pencil to practice skills, and technology (such as graphing calculators, spreadsheets, or geometry software) to investigate more complicated mathematical ideas.

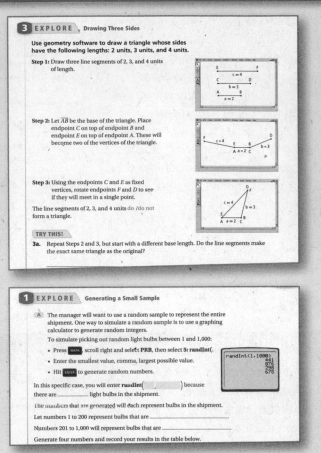

3 EXPLORE   Drawing Three Sides

Use geometry software to draw a triangle whose sides have the following lengths: 2 units, 3 units, and 4 units.

Step 1: Draw three line segments of 2, 3, and 4 units of length.

Step 2: Let $\overline{AB}$ be the base of the triangle. Place endpoint C on top of endpoint B and endpoint E on top of endpoint A. These will become two of the vertices of the triangle.

Step 3: Using the endpoints C and E as fixed vertices, rotate endpoints F and D to see if they will meet in a single point.

The line segments of 2, 3, and 4 units do /do not form a triangle.

TRY THIS!

3a. Repeat Steps 2 and 3, but start with a different base length. Do the line segments make the exact same triangle as the original?

1 EXPLORE   Generating a Small Sample

A The manager will want to use a random sample to represent the entire shipment. One way to simulate a random sample is to use a graphing calculator to generate random integers.

To simulate picking out random light bulbs between 1 and 1,000:

- Press [MATH], scroll right and select **PRB**, then select **5: randInt(.**
- Enter the smallest value, comma, largest possible value.
- Hit [ENTER] to generate random numbers.

In this specific case, you will enter **randInt**(_____ , _____) because there are _____ light bulbs in the shipment.

The numbers that are generated will each represent bulbs in the shipment.

Let numbers 1 to 200 represent bulbs that are _____

Numbers 201 to 1,000 will represent bulbs that are _____

Generate four numbers and record your results in the table below.

6 Attend to precision.

Precision refers not only to the correctness of arithmetic calculations, algebraic manipulations, and geometric reasoning but also to the proper use of mathematical language, symbols, and units to communicate mathematical ideas. Throughout *On Core Mathematics Grade 7* you will demonstrate your skills in these areas when you are asked to calculate, describe, show, explain, prove, and predict.

5. A train travels at 72 miles per hour. Will the graph of the train's rate of speed show that the relationship between the number of miles traveled and the number of hours is a proportional relationship? Explain.

The graph shows the relationship between time and the distance run by two horses.

6. How long does it take each horse to run 1 mile?   Horse Training

6. Reasoning A composite figure is formed by combining a square and a triangle. Its total area is 32.5 ft². The area of the triangle is 7.5 ft². What is the length of each side of the square?

REFLECT

1a. *Theoretical probability* is a way to describe how you found the chance of winning a MP3 player in the scenario above. Using the spinner example to help you, explain in your own words how to find the theoretical probability of an event.

1b. Suppose you choose Spinner A. What is the probability that you will not win? Show

In *On Core Mathematics Grade 7*, you will look for patterns or regularity in mathematical structures such as expressions, equations, operations, geometric figures, and diagrams. You will use these patterns to generalize beyond a specific case and to make connections between related problems.

2 EXAMPLE Identifying Proportional Relationships

An Internet café charges a one-time $5 service fee and then $2 for every hour of use. Is this relationship a proportional relationship?

A Complete the table.

Time (h)	1	2	5		8
Total Cost ($)	7			17	

B Plot the data from the table and connect the points with a line.

C The graph of the data is a _____

The line does/does not go through the origin.

So, the relationship is _____

Internet Café Charges

TRY THIS!

2a. Plot the data from the table and connect the

Canon Rental Fee

---

1 EXPLORE Measuring Angles

A Using a ruler, draw a pair of intersecting lines. Label each angle from 1 to 4.

B Use a protractor to help you complete the chart.

Angle	Measure of Angle
m∠1	
m∠2	
m∠3	
m∠4	
m∠1 + m∠2	
m∠2 + m∠3	
m∠3 + m∠4	
m∠4 + m∠1	

REFLECT

1a. Conjecture Share your results with other students. Make a conjecture about pairs of angles that are opposite of each other. Make a conjecture about pairs of angles that are next to each other.

---

1 EXPLORE Exploring Circumference

A Use a measuring tape to find the circumference of five circular objects. Then measure the distance across each item to find its diameter. Record the measurements of each object in the table below.

Object	Circumference C	Diameter d	$\frac{C}{d}$

B Divide the circumference of each object by its diameter. Round your answer to the nearest hundredth.

C Describe what you notice about the ratio $\frac{C}{d}$ in your table.

REFLECT

1a. Conjecture Compare

The Number System

Unit Focus

In this unit, you will learn how to recognize rational numbers. You will convert rational numbers to their equivalent decimal form. You will also learn how to add, subtract, multiply, and divide rational numbers that are positive and negative, and you will solve multi-step problems that involve rational numbers.

Unit at a Glance

COMMON CORE

UNIT 1

Unpacking the Common Core State Standards

Use the table to help you understand the Standards for Mathematical Content that are taught in this unit. Refer to the lessons listed after each standard for exploration and practice.

COMMON CORE Standards for Mathematical Content	What It Means For You
7.NS.1 Apply and extend previous understandings of addition and subtraction to ... rational numbers.... **7.NS.1a** Describe situations in which opposite quantities combine to make 0. **7.NS.1b** Understand $p + q$ as the number located a distance $|q|$ from p, in the positive or negative direction depending on whether q is positive or negative. Show that a number and its opposite have a sum of 0 (are additive inverses). Interpret sums of rational numbers by describing real-world contexts. **7.NS.1c** Understand subtraction of rational numbers as adding the additive inverse, $p - q = p + (-q)$. Show that the distance between two rational numbers on the number line is the absolute value of their difference, and apply this principle in real-world contexts. **7.NS.1d** Apply properties of operations as strategies to add and subtract rational numbers. Lessons 1-2, 1-3	You will learn how to add and subtract rational numbers with the same sign and with different signs. You will learn that subtracting a rational number is the same as adding its additive inverse.
7.NS.2 Apply and extend previous understandings of multiplication and division ...to...rational numbers. **7.NS.2a** Understand that multiplication is extended from fractions to rational numbers by requiring that operations continue to satisfy the properties of operations, particularly the distributive property, leading to products such as $(-1)(-1) = 1$ and the rules for multiplying signed numbers. Interpret products of rational numbers by describing real-world contexts. **7.NS.2b** Understand that integers can be divided, provided that the divisor is not zero, and every quotient of integers (with non-zero divisor) is a rational number. If p and q are integers, then $-\left(\frac{p}{q}\right) = \frac{(-p)}{q} = \frac{p}{(-q)}$. Interpret quotients of rational numbers by describing real-world contexts. **7.NS.2c** Apply properties of operations as strategies to multiply and divide rational numbers. Lessons 1-4, 1-5	You will multiply and divide positive and negative rational numbers. You will solve real-world applications with multiplication and division of rational numbers. You will explore the meaning of division by 0.

Rational Numbers and Decimals

COMMON CORE

CC.7.NS.2d

Essential question: *How can you convert a rational number to a decimal?*

A **rational number** is a number that can be written as a ratio of two integers a and b, where b is not zero. For example, $\frac{4}{7}$ is a rational number, as is 0.37 because it can be written as the fraction $\frac{37}{100}$.

1 EXPLORE   Describing Decimal Forms of Rational Numbers

A Use a calculator to find the equivalent decimal form of each fraction. Remember that numbers that repeat can be written as 0.333... or $0.\overline{3}$.

Fraction	$\frac{1}{4}$	$\frac{5}{8}$	$\frac{2}{3}$	$\frac{2}{9}$	$\frac{12}{5}$		
Decimal Equivalent						0.2	0.875

B Now find the corresponding fraction of the decimal equivalents given in the last two columns in the table. Write the fractions in simplest form.

C **Conjecture** What do you notice about the digits after the decimal point in the decimal forms of the fractions? Compare notes with your neighbor and refine your conjecture if necessary.

_____

REFLECT

1a. Consider the decimal 0.10100100010000100000I... Do you think this decimal represents a rational number? Why or why not?

_____

_____

1b. Do you think a negative sign affects whether or not a number is a rational number? Use $-\frac{8}{5}$ as an example.

_____

_____

1c. Do you think a mixed number is a rational number? Explain.

_____

_____

You can convert a rational number to a decimal using long division.

2 EXAMPLE Writing Rational Numbers as Decimals Using Long Division

Write each rational number as a decimal.

A $\frac{5}{16}$

Divide 5 by 16.
Add a zero after the decimal point.
Subtract 48 from 50.
Use the grid to help you complete the long division.

Add zeros in the dividend and continue dividing
until the remainder is 0.

				0.	3			
1	6	)	5.	0				
			−4	8				

The decimal equivalent of $\frac{5}{16}$ is _____.

B $\frac{1}{11}$

Divide 1 by 11.
Add a zero after the decimal point.
10 can be divided by 11 zero times.
Use the grid to help you complete the long division.

You can stop dividing once you discover a repeating
pattern in the quotient.

Write the quotient with its repeating pattern and
indicate that the repeating numbers continue.

			0.	0			
1	1	)	1.	0			
			−0				

The decimal equivalent of $\frac{1}{11}$ is _____.

REFLECT

2a. Do you think that decimals that have repeating patterns always
have the same number of digits in their pattern? Explain.

_____

_____

_____

3 EXAMPLE Writing Mixed Numbers as Decimals

Yvonne bought $4\frac{7}{8}$ yards of material to make a dress. Write $4\frac{7}{8}$ as a decimal.

Step 1: Write $4\frac{7}{8}$ as an improper fraction.

$$4\frac{7}{8} = \underline{\quad\quad}$$

Step 2: Divide the numerator by the denominator.

$$8\overline{)39.}$$

The decimal equivalent of $4\frac{7}{8}$ is _____.

Is the decimal equivalent a terminating or repeating decimal? _____

TRY THIS!

3a. Yvonne made $2\frac{3}{4}$ quarts of punch. Write $2\frac{3}{4}$ as a decimal.

$$2\frac{3}{4} = \underline{\quad\quad}$$

Is the decimal equivalent a terminating or repeating decimal?

_____

3b. Yvonne bought a watermelon that weighed $3\frac{1}{3}$ pounds. Write $3\frac{1}{3}$ as a decimal.

$$3\frac{1}{3} = \underline{\quad\quad}$$

Is the decimal equivalent a terminating or repeating decimal?

_____

REFLECT

3c. Look at the decimal 0.121122111222... If the pattern continues, is this a repeating decimal? Explain.

_____

_____

PRACTICE

Write each rational number as a decimal. Then tell whether each decimal is a terminating or a repeating decimal.

1. $\frac{3}{5} =$ _____

2. $\frac{89}{100} =$ _____

3. $\frac{4}{12} =$ _____

4. $\frac{25}{99} =$ _____

5. $\frac{7}{9} =$ _____

6. $\frac{9}{25} =$ _____

7. $\frac{1}{25} =$ _____

8. $\frac{25}{176} =$ _____

9. $\frac{12}{1,000} =$ _____

Write each mixed number as a decimal.

10. $11\frac{1}{6} =$ _____

11. $8\frac{23}{100} =$ _____

12. $54\frac{3}{11} =$ _____

13. $2\frac{9}{10} =$ _____

14. $7\frac{3}{15} =$ _____

15. $3\frac{1}{18} =$ _____

16. $7\frac{2}{5} =$ _____

17. $12\frac{9}{150} =$ _____

18. $10\frac{11}{40} =$ _____

19. Maggie bought $3\frac{2}{3}$ lb of apples to make some apple pies. What is the weight of the apples written as a decimal?

$3\frac{2}{3} =$ _____

20. Harry's dog weighs $12\frac{7}{8}$ pounds. What is Harry's dog's weight written as a decimal?

$12\frac{7}{8} =$ _____

21. Philip has an MP3 player that weighs $4\frac{9}{10}$ oz. What is the weight of the MP3 player written as a decimal?

$4\frac{9}{10} =$ _____

22. Mari bought $124\frac{7}{20}$ feet of fabric to make some curtains. What is the length of the fabric written as a decimal?

$124\frac{7}{20} =$ _____

23. **Critical Thinking** Tom is trying to write $\frac{3}{47}$ as a decimal. He used long division and divided until he got the quotient 0.0638297872, at which point he stopped. Since the decimal doesn't seem to terminate or repeat, he concluded that $\frac{3}{47}$ is not rational. Do you agree or disagree? Why?

_____

_____

_____

_____

Adding Rational Numbers

Essential question: *How can you add rational numbers?*

1 **E X A M P L E** Adding Rational Numbers with the Same Sign

A Andrea has 6 cups of fruit punch in a bowl. She adds 3 cups of fruit punch to the bowl. How many cups of punch are there altogether?

Find $6 + 3$.
Start at 6.
Move $|3| = 3$ units to the *right* because the second addend is *positive*.

The result is _____.

There are _____ cups of punch.

B Kyle pours out $\frac{3}{4}$ cup of milk from a pitcher. Then he pours out another $\frac{1}{2}$ cup from the pitcher. How many cups of milk does he pour out altogether?

Use negative numbers to represent amounts that are poured out of the pitcher.

Find $-\frac{3}{4} + \left(-\frac{1}{2}\right)$. Start at $-\frac{3}{4}$.

Move $\left|-\frac{1}{2}\right| = \frac{1}{2}$ unit to the *left* because the second addend is *negative*.

The result is _____.

Kyle pours out _____ cups.

TRY THIS!

Use a number line to find each sum.

1a. $3 + 1\frac{1}{2} =$ _____

1b. $-2.5 + (-4.5) =$ _____

REFLECT

1c. **Conjecture** Work with other students to make a conjecture about the sign of the sum when the addends have the same sign.

_____

_____

To add two rational numbers with the same sign, find the sum of their absolute values. Then use the same sign as the sign of the two rational numbers.

2 EXAMPLE   Adding Rational Numbers with Different Signs

A   **A football team gains 4 yards on their first play. Then they lose 7 yards on their next play. What is the team's overall gain or loss on the two plays?**

Use a positive number to represent a gain and a negative number to represent a loss.

Find $4 + (-7)$.

Start at 4.

Move $|-7| = 7$ units to the _____

because the second addend is _____ .

The result is _____ .

The team gains / loses _____ yards.

B   **Ernesto writes a check for \$2.50. Then he deposits \$6 in his checking account. What is the overall increase or decrease in the account's balance?**

Use a positive number to represent a deposit and a negative number to represent a withdrawal or a check.

Find $-2.5 + 6$.

Start at -2.5.

Move $|6| = 6$ units to the _____

because the second addend is _____ .

The result is _____ .

The account balance increases / decreases by \$_____ .

TRY THIS!

Use a number line to find each sum.

2a. $-8 + 5 =$ _____

2b. $\frac{1}{2} + \left(-\frac{3}{4}\right) =$ _____

REFLECT

2c.   **Conjecture** Work with other students to make a conjecture about the sign of the sum when the addends have different signs.

_____

_____

_____

To add two rational numbers with different signs, find the difference of their absolute values. Then use the sign of the rational number with the greater absolute value.

3 EXAMPLE   Finding the Additive Inverse

A   **Abby takes 5 gallons of water out of an aquarium. Later, she adds 5 gallons of water to the aquarium. What is the overall increase or decrease in the amount of water in the aquarium?**

Use a positive number to represent water added to the aquarium and a negative number to represent water taken out of the aquarium.

Find $-5 + 5$. Start at _____.

Move $|5| = 5$ units to the _____

because the second addend is _____.

The result is _____.

This means _____.

B   **Kendrick adds $\frac{3}{4}$ cup of chicken stock to a pot. Then he takes $\frac{3}{4}$ cup of stock out of the pot. What is the overall increase or decrease in the amount of chicken stock in the pot?**

Use a positive number to represent chicken stock added to the pot and a negative number to represent chicken stock taken out of the pot.

Find $\frac{3}{4} + \left(-\frac{3}{4}\right)$. Start at _____.

Move $\left|-\frac{3}{4}\right| = \frac{3}{4}$ units to the _____

because the second addend is _____.

The result is _____.

This means _____.

REFLECT

3a.   Conjecture Work with other students to make a conjecture about the sum of a number and its opposite.

_____

3b.   What is the opposite of 50? What is the opposite of -75?

_____

The **opposite**, or **additive inverse**, of a number is the same distance from 0 on a number line as the original number, but on the other side of 0. The sum of a number and its additive inverse is 0. Zero is its own additive inverse.

PRACTICE

Use a number line to find each sum.

1. $3 + (-8) =$ ___ -5 ___

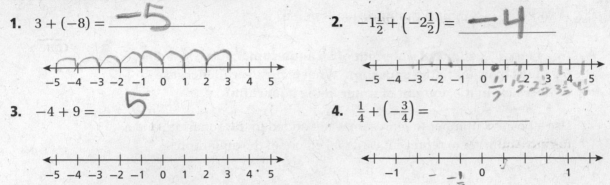

2. $-1\frac{1}{2} + \left(-2\frac{1}{2}\right) =$ ___ -4 ___

3. $-4 + 9 =$ ___ 5 ___

4. $\frac{1}{4} + \left(-\frac{3}{4}\right) =$ ___

Tell what sum is modeled on each number line. Then find the sum.

5.

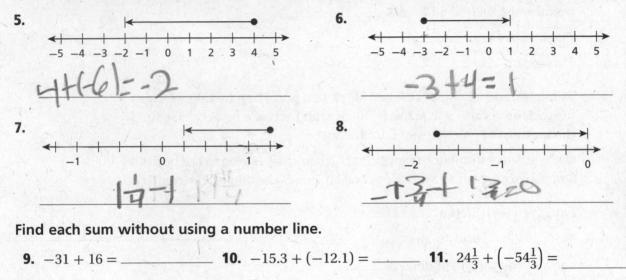

$4 + (-6) = -2$

6.

$-3 + 4 = 1$

7.

$1\frac{1}{4} + 1$

8.

$-1\frac{3}{4} + 1\frac{3}{4} = 0$

Find each sum without using a number line.

9. $-31 + 16 =$ ___

10. $-15.3 + (-12.1) =$ ___

11. $24\frac{1}{3} + \left(-54\frac{1}{3}\right) =$ ___

12. $-40 + (-18) + 40 =$ ___

13. $15 + (-22) + 9 =$ ___

14. $-1 + 1 + (-25) =$ ___

15. Describe a real-world situation that can be represented by the expression $-10 + (-2)$. Then find the sum and explain what it represents in terms of the situation.

___

___

16. A contestant on a game show has 30 points. She answers a question correctly to win 15 points. Then she answers a question incorrectly and loses 25 points. What is the contestant's final score?

___

17. **Error Analysis** A student evaluated $-4 + x$ for $x = -9$ and got an answer of 5. What might the student have done wrong?

___

___

Subtracting Rational Numbers

Essential question: *How do you subtract rational numbers?*

COMMON
CORE

CC.7.NS.1c,
CC.7.NS.1d

1 EXPLORE Subtracting Rational Numbers

A **The temperature on Monday was 5 °C. The temperature on Thursday was 7 degrees less than the temperature on Monday. What was the temperature on Thursday?**

Subtract to find Thursday's temperature.
Find $5 - 7$. Start at 5.
Move $|7| = 7$ units to the *left* because you are subtracting a *positive* number.

```
←+——+——+——+——+——+——+——+——+——+——+→
 −5 −4 −3 −2 −1  0  1  2  3  4  5
```

The result is _____.
The temperature on Thursday was _____ °C.

B **The temperature on Friday was −7 °C. The temperature on Sunday was −4 °C. How many degrees did the temperature change from Friday to Sunday?**

Subtract to find the difference in temperature.
Find $-4 - (-7)$. Start at −4.
Move $|7| = 7$ units to the *right* because you are subtracting a *negative* number.

```
←+——+——+——+——+——+——+——+——+——+——+→
 −5 −4 −3 −2 −1  0  1  2  3  4  5
```

The result is _____.

The temperature change from Friday to Sunday was _____ °C.

TRY THIS!

Use a number line to find each difference.

1a. $-6 - 2 =$ _____

1b. $1\frac{1}{2} - (-2) =$ _____

```
←+——+——+——+——+——+——+——+——+——+——+→
 −10 −9 −8 −7 −6 −5 −4 −3 −2 −1  0
```

```
←+——+——+——+——+——+——+——+——+——+——+→
   −1    0    1    2    3    4
```

REFLECT

1c. Work with other students to compare addition of negative numbers on a number line to subtraction of negative numbers on a number line.

_____

_____

2 EXPLORE   Adding the Opposite

A **Joe is diving 2 feet below sea level. He decides to descend 7 more feet. How many feet below sea level is he?**

Use negative numbers to represent the number of feet below sea level.

Find $-2 - 7$.
Start at -2.
Move $|7| = 7$ units to the _____

because you are subtracting a _____ number.

The result is _____ . Joe is _____ feet below sea level.

B **Marianne wrote a check for $2. She then withdrew $7 from her checking account at the bank. How much did Marianne take out of her checking account?**

Use negative numbers to represent amounts of money Marianne took out of her checking account.

Find $-2 + (-7)$.
Start at -2.
Move $|-7| = 7$ units to the _____

because you are adding a _____ number.

The result is _____ . Marianne withdrew _____ .

TRY THIS!

Use a number line to find each difference or sum.

2a. $-3 - 3 =$ _____

2b. $-3 + (-3) =$ _____

REFLECT

2c. Compare the results from **2a** and **2b**.

_____

2d. Work with other students to make a conjecture about how to change a subtraction problem into an addition problem.

_____

_____

To subtract a number, add its opposite. This can also be written as $p - q = p + (-q)$.

A cave explorer climbed from an elevation of −11 meters to an elevation of −5 meters. What vertical distance did the explorer climb?

There are two ways to find the vertical distance.

A   Start at __−11__.

Count the number of units on the vertical number line up to −5.

The explorer climbed __6__ meters.

This means that the vertical distance between

−11 meters and −5 meters is __6__ meters.

B   Find the difference between the two elevations and use absolute value to find the distance.

$-11 - (-5) =$ __−6__.

Take the absolute value of the difference because distance traveled is always a nonnegative number.

$|-11 - (-5)| =$ __−6__.

The vertical distance is __−6__ meters.

```
  0
 −1
 −2
 −3
 −4
 −5
 −6
 −7
 −8
 −9
−10
−11 →
```

REFLECT

3a.   Does it matter which way you subtract the values when finding distance? Explain.

Ending − beginnig, -5-(-11)=6

3b.   Would the same methods work if both the numbers were positive? What if one of the numbers were positive and the other negative?

I would work both ways, but it wouldn't matter, it would be 6 still.

The distance between two values a and b on a number line is represented by the absolute value of the difference of a and b.

Distance between a and $b = |a-b|$ or $|b-a|$.

PRACTICE

Use a number line to find each difference.

1. $5 - (-8) =$ ___13___

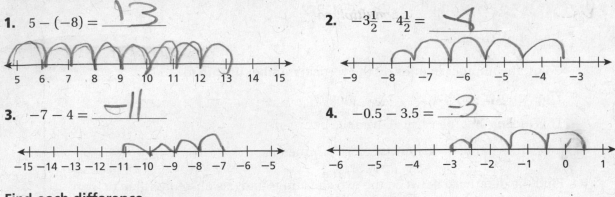

2. $-3\frac{1}{2} - 4\frac{1}{2} =$ ___-4___

3. $-7 - 4 =$ ___-11___

4. $-0.5 - 3.5 =$ ___-3___

Find each difference.

5. $-14 - 22 =$ ___-36___

6. $-12.5 - (-4.8) =$ ___8.7___
-4.8

7. $\frac{1}{3} - \left(-\frac{2}{3}\right) =$ ___1___
                                          3

8. $65 - (-14) =$ ___71___

9. $-\frac{2}{9} - (-3) =$ _____

10. $24\frac{3}{8} - \left(-54\frac{1}{8}\right) =$ ___$78\frac{4}{8}$___

11. A girl is snorkeling 1 meter below sea level and then dives down another 0.5 meter. How far below seal level is the girl?

$-1 + -0.5 = 1.5$

12. The first play of a football game resulted in a loss of 12 yards. Then a penalty resulted in another loss of 5 yards. What is the total loss or gain?

loss $-12 + -5 = -17$

13. A climber starts descending from 533 feet above sea level and keeps going until she reaches 10 feet below sea level. How many feet did she descend?

$-533 - (-10) = 523 ft$

14. The temperature on Sunday was $-15\,°C$. The temperature on Monday was 12 degrees less than the temperature on Sunday. What was the temperature on Monday?

$-15 + -12 = 27°C$

15. The lowest temperature on Thursday was $-20\,°C$. The lowest temperature on Saturday was $-12\,°C$. What was the difference between the lowest temperatures?

$20 - (-12) = -8$

16. Eleni withdrew $45.00 from her savings account. She then used her debit card to buy groceries for $30.15. What was the total amount Eleni took out of her account?

17. On a number line, what is the distance between -61.5 and -23.4?

Multiplying Rational Numbers

COMMON CORE

CC.7.NS.2a,
CC.7.NS.2c

Essential question: *How do you multiply rational numbers?*

1 EXPLORE   Multiplying Rational Numbers

A **Henry made three withdrawals of $2 each from his savings account. How much did he withdraw altogether?**

Find 3(−2).

Start at 0. Move 2 units to the left three times because 3(−2)

means (−2) + _____ + _____.

The result is _____.

Henry withdrew _____ from his savings account.

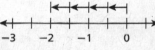

+(−2) +(−2) +(−2)

−8 −7 −6 −5 −4 −3 −2 −1 0

B **Gina hiked down a mountain in $\frac{1}{2}$-mile sections. She hiked 4 sections. How many miles did she hike down?**

Find $\left(-\frac{1}{2}\right)4$.

You can use the Commutative Property of Multiplication

to write $\left(-\frac{1}{2}\right)4$ as _____.

Move $\frac{1}{2}$ unit to the left 4 times.

The result is _____.

Gina hiked down _____ miles.

−3   −2   −1   0

C **Find the product of −4 and −3.**

Write (−4)(−3) as −4(−3), which means the *opposite* of 4(−3).

First, the product of 4(−3) can be modeled as 4 groups of _____.

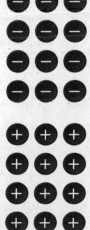

Then flip the counters over to find the opposite of 4(−3).

(−4)(−3) = _____

The model shows that the product of two negative numbers is positive.

D Identify a possible pattern. Use the pattern to find the next three products.

$$-5(3) \quad = -15$$
$$-5(2) \quad = -10$$
$$-5(1) \quad = -5$$
$$-5(0) \quad = 0$$
$$-5(-1) = 5$$
$$-5(-2) = \rule{3cm}{0.4pt}$$
$$-5(-3) = \rule{3cm}{0.4pt}$$
$$-5(-4) = \rule{3cm}{0.4pt}$$

Find the pattern in the products. Make your observations starting from the top of the list of equations and going down.

The factor of _____ is always the same.

The second factor that is being multiplied by –5 increases / decreases in each equation. By how much? _____

The product of the factors increases / decreases in each equation.

By how much? _____

Does this pattern hold true for the first 5 equations? _____

A pattern for these equations is: If you increases / decreases the second

factor by _____ the product increases / decreases by _____.

Complete the pattern.

REFLECT

1a. What do you notice about the product of two rational numbers with different signs? What do you notice about the product of two rational numbers with the same sign?

_____

_____

1b. In **D** , would the products change if you made your observations starting at the bottom of the list of equations and went up? Would the pattern change?

_____

_____

TRY THIS!

Find each product.

1c. $2(-12) = $ _____   **1d.** $\left(-\frac{2}{3}\right)\left(-\frac{5}{6}\right) = $ _____   **1e.** $(-7)(7.8) = $ _____

The numerical properties that work for positive rational numbers (such as the Distributive Property) must also be true for negative rational numbers. For the properties to work with all rational numbers, the product of two negative numbers must be positive. You can see that this is true using algebra.

Start with something you know about positive and negative numbers:

$$1 + (-1) = 0$$

Use this to write an equation using the Distributive Property:

$-1[1 + (-1)]$	$=$	$-1(1)$	$+$	$(-1)(-1)$	Distribute.
You know that $1 + (-1) = 0$.		You know that $(-1)(1) = -1$.		You don't know the value of $(-1)(-1)$, so call it x for now.	

$-1(0)$	$=$	-1	$+$	x	
0	$=$	-1	$+$	x	Simplify.
1	$=$	x			Addition Property of Equality
1	$=$	$(-1)(-1)$			Substitute.

So, $(-1)(-1) = 1$. The product of two negative numbers is positive.

The rules for the signs of products of rational numbers can be summarized. Let p and q be rational numbers.

Products of Rational Numbers

Sign of Factor p	Sign of Factor q	Sign of Product pq
+	−	−
−	+	−
+	+	+
−	−	+

Properties of Zero

p	q	Product pq
0	+/−	0
+/−	0	0

PRACTICE

Find each product.

1. $-1(9) =$ ___ -9 ___
2. $\left(-\frac{2}{5}\right)\left(-\frac{12}{7}\right) =$ ___ $\frac{24}{35}$ ___
3. $(-9)(-6) =$ ___ 54 ___
4. $-2(50) =$ ___ -100 ___
5. $(-4)(15) =$ ___ -60 ___
6. $(3)(-52.4) =$ ___ -157.2 ___
7. $(6)\left(-\frac{7}{15}\right) =$ ___ $\frac{14}{5} = 2\frac{4}{5}$ ___
8. $\left(-\frac{19}{9}\right)(0) =$ ___ 0 ___
9. $(8)(-12) =$ ___ -96 ___

10. Flora made 7 withdrawals of $75 each from her bank account. How much did she withdraw in total?

   $525.00

11. Each of a football team's 3 plays resulted in a loss of 5 yards. How many yards in total did they lose in the 3 plays?

   -15 yards

12. The temperature dropped 2 °F every hour for 6 hours. What was the total number of degrees the temperature dropped in the 6 hours?

   -8°F

13. A mountain climber climbed down a cliff $\frac{1}{4}$ mile at a time. He did this 5 times in one day. How many miles did he climb down?

   -1.25 miles

14. The price of one share of Acme Company declined $3.50 per day for 4 days in a row. How much did the price of one share decline in total after the 4 days?

   $14.00

15. In one day, 18 people each withdrew $100 from an ATM machine. How much money was withdrawn from the ATM machine?

   $1800.00

16. Describe a real-world situation that can be represented by the product $(-34)(3)$. Then find the product and explain what the product means in terms of the real-world situation.

   A mountain climber is at 3 ft. before the top. He went down 34 times more than he was before. Where on the mountain is he now? -102 ft. He is 102 ft below surface

Dividing Rational Numbers

Essential question: *How do you divide rational numbers?*

1 EXPLORE Dividing Integers

A diver needs to descend to a depth of 100 feet. She wants to do it in 5 equal descents. How far should she travel in each descent?

A To solve this problem, you can set up a division problem: $\dfrac{-100}{} = ?$

B Rewrite the division problem as a multiplication problem.
Think: Some number multiplied by 5 equals -100.

$\underline{\hspace{2cm}} \times \,? = -100$

C Remember the rules for integer multiplication. If the product is negative, one of the factors must be negative. Since _____ is positive, the unknown factor must be positive / negative.

D You know that $5 \times \underline{\hspace{1.5cm}} = 100$. So, using the rules for integer multiplication you can say that $5 \times \underline{\hspace{1.5cm}} = -100$.

The diver should descend _____ feet in each descent.

TRY THIS!

Find each quotient.

1a. $\dfrac{14}{-7} = $ _____   **1b.** $\dfrac{-36}{-9} = $ _____   **1c.** $\dfrac{-55}{11} = $ _____   **1d.** $\dfrac{-45}{-5} = $ _____

REFLECT

1e. What do you notice about the quotient of two rational numbers with different signs?

_____

_____

1f. What do you notice about the quotient of two rational numbers with the same sign? Does it matter if both signs are positive or both are negative?

_____

_____

Quotients can have negative signs in different places.

Are the rational numbers $\frac{12}{-4}$, $\frac{-12}{4}$, and $-\left(\frac{12}{4}\right)$ equivalent?

A Find each quotient. Then use the rules you found in **1** to make sure the sign of the quotient is correct.

$\frac{12}{-4} = $ _____ $\frac{-12}{4} = $ _____ $-\left(\frac{12}{4}\right) = $ _____

B What do you notice about each quotient?

_____

C The rational numbers are / are not equivalent.

D **Conjecture** Explain how the placement of the negative sign in the rational number affects the sign of the quotients.

_____

_____

TRY THIS!

Write equivalent expressions for each quotient.

2a. $\frac{14}{-7}$, _____ , _____   **2b.** $\frac{-32}{-8}$, _____ , _____   **2c.** $\frac{-99}{9}$, _____ , _____

---

3 EXAMPLE   Quotients of Rational Numbers

Find each quotient.

A $\dfrac{\frac{3}{8}}{-\frac{1}{4}}$

The quotient will be negative / positive because the signs are _____.

To find the quotient, rewrite as $\frac{3}{8} \times$ _____.

$\frac{3}{8} \times \boxed{} = \boxed{}$

$= \boxed{}$

$\dfrac{\frac{3}{8}}{-\frac{1}{4}} = \boxed{}$

Find each quotient.

B $\dfrac{-5.6}{-1.4}$

The quotient will be negative / positive because the signs are _____.

Divide.

$\dfrac{-5.6}{-1.4} =$ _____

> **TRY THIS!**
>
> **Find each quotient.**
>
> **3a.** $\dfrac{2.8}{-4} =$ _____   **3b.** $\dfrac{-\dfrac{5}{8}}{-\dfrac{6}{7}} =$ _____   **3c.** $-\dfrac{5.5}{0.5} =$ _____

You used the relationship between multiplication and division to find the sign of quotients. You can use multiplication to understand why division by zero is not possible.

Consider the division problem $5 \div 0 = ?$. Write a related multiplication problem: $0 \times ? = 5$. This multiplication sentence says that there is some number times 0 that equals 5. You already know that 0 times any number equals 0. This means division by 0 is not possible, so we say that division by 0 is undefined.

The rules for the signs of quotients of rational numbers can be summarized. Let p and q be rational numbers.

Quotients of Rational Numbers

Sign of Factor p	Sign of Factor q	Sign of Quotient $\frac{p}{q}$
+	−	−
−	+	−
+	+	+
−	−	+

Properties of Zero

p	q	Quotient $\frac{p}{q}$
0	+/−	0
+/−	0	Undefined

Also, $-\left(\dfrac{p}{q}\right) = \dfrac{-p}{q} = \dfrac{p}{-q}$, for q not zero.

Find each quotient.

1. $\dfrac{0.72}{-0.9} =$ _____

2. $-\left(\dfrac{\frac{1}{5}}{\frac{7}{5}}\right) =$ _____

3. $\dfrac{56}{-7} =$ _____

4. $\dfrac{251}{4} \div \left(-\dfrac{3}{8}\right) =$ _____

5. $\dfrac{75}{-\frac{1}{5}} =$ _____

6. $\dfrac{-91}{-13} =$ _____

7. $\dfrac{-\frac{3}{7}}{\frac{9}{4}} =$ _____

8. $-\dfrac{12}{0.03} =$ _____

9. $\dfrac{0.65}{-0.5} =$ _____

10. $\dfrac{5}{-\frac{2}{8}} =$ _____

11. $5\frac{1}{3} \div \left(-1\frac{1}{2}\right) =$ _____

12. $\dfrac{-120}{-6} =$ _____

13. The price of one share of ABC Company declined a total of $45 in 5 days. How much did the price of one share decline, on average, per day?

_____

14. A mountain climber explored a cliff that is 225 yards high in 5 equal descents. How many yards was one descent?

_____

15. Describe a real-world situation that can be represented by the quotient −85 ÷ 15. Then find the quotient and explain what the quotient means in terms of the real-world situation.

_____

_____

_____

16. Divide 5 by 4. Is your answer a rational number? Explain.

_____

_____

17. **Critical Thinking** Should the quotient of an integer divided by a non-zero integer always be a rational number? Why or why not?

_____

_____

Solving Problems with Rational Numbers

Essential question: *How do you solve multi-step problems with rational numbers?*

1 EXPLORE Adding and Subtracting Rational Numbers

Tomas works as an underwater photographer. He starts at a depth of 20 feet, ascends 9 feet, descends 12 feet, and then descends 15 feet more. Write and simplify an expression to find his final depth.

A Write an expression to solve this problem.

Tomas starts at –20 / 20 feet.

When the diver ascends, you add / subtract that distance.

When the diver descends, you add / subtract that distance.

B Write an expression.

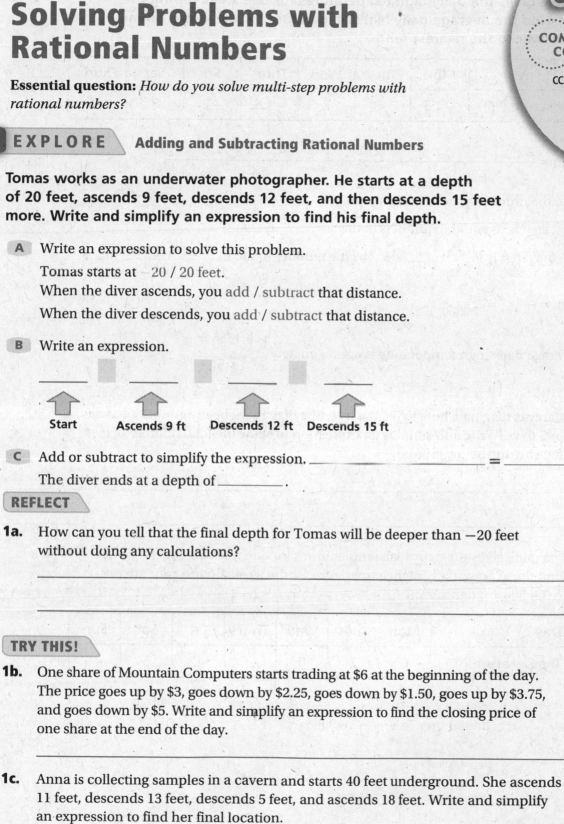

Start   Ascends 9 ft   Descends 12 ft   Descends 15 ft

C Add or subtract to simplify the expression. _____ = _____

The diver ends at a depth of _____ .

REFLECT

1a. How can you tell that the final depth for Tomas will be deeper than −20 feet without doing any calculations?

_____

_____

TRY THIS!

1b. One share of Mountain Computers starts trading at $6 at the beginning of the day. The price goes up by $3, goes down by $2.25, goes down by $1.50, goes up by $3.75, and goes down by $5. Write and simplify an expression to find the closing price of one share at the end of the day.

_____

1c. Anna is collecting samples in a cavern and starts 40 feet underground. She ascends 11 feet, descends 13 feet, descends 5 feet, and ascends 18 feet. Write and simplify an expression to find her final location.

_____

The table gives the daily high temperatures for one week during the winter. Find the average daily high temperature for the week. Round your answer to the nearest tenth.

Day	Mon	Tues	Wed	Thurs	Fri	Sat	Sun
Temperature (°F)	−4.5	−3	2	−1.5	−2	3	−5

$$\text{Average} = \frac{-4.5 + -3 + 2 + -1.5 + -2 + 3 + -5}{7}$$

You use the order of operations to simplify.

The first step is to add the numbers in the ~~the~~ *numerato* _____.

The second step is to *divide* by the number in the *numerator* _____.

$$\text{Average} = \frac{-14}{7} = 2$$

The average daily high temperature is approximately *2°F* _____.

> **TRY THIS!**

2a. Marcy is digging a hole to plant a tree. She digs 1 foot below ground each day for 5 days. Write and simplify an expression to show the total number of feet that she dug below ground.

$-1 \times 5 = -5$

2b. The table gives the daily high temperatures for one week during the winter. Find the average daily high temperature for the week. Round your answer to the nearest tenth.

Day	Mon	Tues	Wed	Thurs	Fri	Sat	Sun
Temperature (°F)	6	2	0	−6	−2	5	−5

$6 + 2 + 0 + -6 + -2 + 5 + 5$

$-13 + 13 = 0$°F

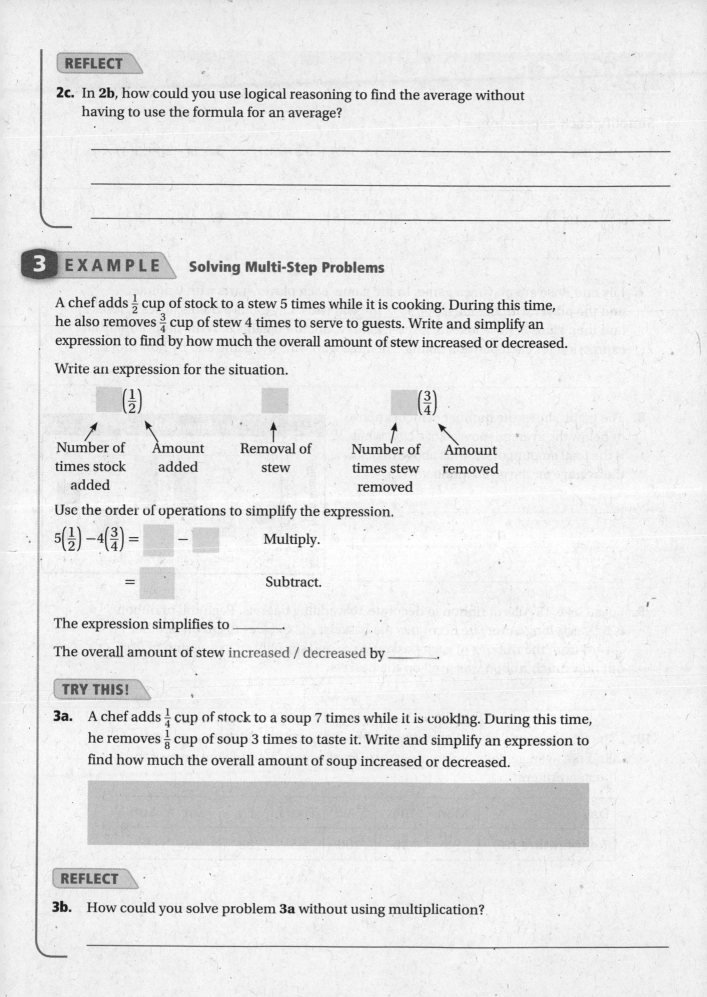

REFLECT

2c. In **2b**, how could you use logical reasoning to find the average without having to use the formula for an average?

_____

_____

_____

3 EXAMPLE Solving Multi-Step Problems

A chef adds $\frac{1}{2}$ cup of stock to a stew 5 times while it is cooking. During this time, he also removes $\frac{3}{4}$ cup of stew 4 times to serve to guests. Write and simplify an expression to find by how much the overall amount of stew increased or decreased.

Write an expression for the situation.

$\left(\frac{1}{2}\right)$ $\left(\frac{3}{4}\right)$

Number of   Amount   Removal of   Number of   Amount
times stock   added   stew   times stew   removed
added   removed

Use the order of operations to simplify the expression.

$5\left(\frac{1}{2}\right) - 4\left(\frac{3}{4}\right) = \boxed{} - \boxed{}$ Multiply.

$= \boxed{}$ Subtract.

The expression simplifies to _____.

The overall amount of stew increased / decreased by _____.

TRY THIS!

3a. A chef adds $\frac{1}{4}$ cup of stock to a soup 7 times while it is cooking. During this time, he removes $\frac{1}{8}$ cup of soup 3 times to taste it. Write and simplify an expression to find how much the overall amount of soup increased or decreased.

REFLECT

3b. How could you solve problem **3a** without using multiplication?

_____

PRACTICE

Simplify each expression.

1. $-2 + 4 + 7 - 5$

2. $-0.25 + 1.78 - 5.9 + 4.1$

3. $5(-2) - 3(4)$

4. $6\left(\frac{7}{8}\right) - 10\left(\frac{4}{5}\right)$

5. $-4\left(\frac{1}{8}\right) - 3\left(\frac{2}{5}\right)$

6. $\frac{1}{2}(6) + 12\left(\frac{1}{6}\right)$

7. Lily and Rose are playing a game. In the game, each player starts with 0 points, and the player with the most points at the end wins. Lily gains 5 points, loses 3, loses 2, and then gains 3. Rose loses 3, loses 4, gains 2, and then gains 3. Write and simplify an expression for each player's points. Then tell who wins the game and by how much.

8. The graph shows the number of inches above or below the average snowfall of a city. What is the total amount of snowfall above or below the average for the given months?

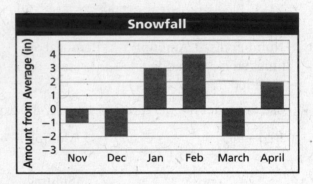

9. Susan uses 15 rolls of ribbon to decorate 10 wedding baskets. Each roll of ribbon is $5\frac{3}{8}$ yards long. After she decorates the baskets, she decides to cut off another $\frac{3}{4}$ yard from the ribbons of each basket. Write and simplify an expression to find out how much ribbon was used on the baskets.

10. The table gives the daily high temperatures for one week during the summer. Find the average daily high temperature for the week. Round your answer to the nearest tenth.

Day	Mon	Tues	Wed	Thurs	Fri	Sat	Sun
Temperature (°F)	98	90	100	95	88	90	97

Problem Solving Connections 🌐

Camp Fun! Waterfall Summer Camp has opened up for the season! Several boys and girls are going this week. You will use addition, subtraction, multiplication, and division of rational numbers to learn about life at camp.

COMMON CORE

CC.7.NS.1
CC.7.NS.2
CC.7.NS.3

1 Cooking

The camp chef is making vegetarian chili for the campers' dinner. The recipe he has serves 6 people. He needs to make this dish for the campers and counselors—a total of 66 people. Help him change the recipe to amounts that will make enough chili for 66 people.

Vegetarian Chili (6 servings)	
$3\frac{1}{2}$ cups stewed tomatoes	$1\frac{1}{3}$ teaspoons ground cumin
$1\frac{3}{4}$ cups salsa	$\frac{3}{8}$ teaspoon salt
2 cups kidney beans	

A Find the new amounts.

B Rewrite the recipe for 66 servings.

Vegetarian Chili (66 servings)	
____ cups stewed tomatoes	____ teaspoons ground cumin
____ cups salsa	____ teaspoons salt
____ cups kidney beans	

2 Weather

Waterfall Summer Camp is located in the mountains and is open from April to October. The table shows average monthly temperatures at the campsite.

Month	Apr	May	Jun	Jul	Aug	Sept	Oct
Temperature (°F)	25	70	65	85	92	82	

A What is the average monthly temperature for the period of April through September? Round your answer to the nearest tenth. Show your work.

B The local newspaper reported that the average monthly temperature for April through September was not typical of the temperatures at the campsite. What do you think is the reason for this? How could you find a more typical representation of the average monthly temperature for the campsite?

C Find a more typical average for the monthly temperature.

D The average monthly temperature from April to October was 70 °F. Find the average temperature for October and write it in the table.

3 Golf

Some of the campers play 9 holes of golf one day. Par, or the expected number of strokes, for the 9-hole course is 32. Every hole has a par value. A golfer's score is the number of strokes above or below par. A golfer's score is above par if he or she takes more strokes than the par value of the hole. A golfer's score is below par if he or she takes fewer strokes than the par value of the hole. A score below par is indicated by a negative number.

Round of 9-Hole Golf							
Golfer	Jan	Sergei	Sue	Yanni	Raz	Leon	Felicity
Score	−6	6	3	−4	2	−3	−5

A Which golfer had the best score? Explain. Now order the players from best score to worst score.

_____

_____

B Which of the golfers have scores that are additive inverses? Explain.

_____

_____

C What is the average score of all the golfers?

D Troy's score is 2 times Leon's score. What is Troy's score?

E Twice the sum of 4 and Yanni's score is Counselor Trina's score. What is Counselor Trina's score?

4 Hiking

The campers go for a hike using the map shown below.

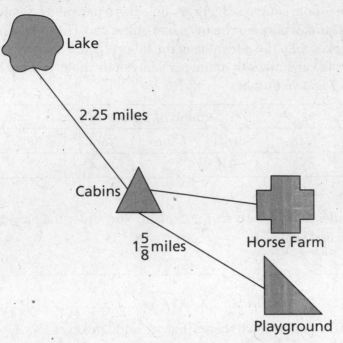

A The distance from the cabins to the horse farm is one-third of the distance from the lake to the playground. How would you find the distance from the cabins to the horse farm?

B How far is it from the cabins to the horse farm?

C Junie walks from the cabins to the lake and back. She then walks to the playground and back. She does each trip twice a week. How much does she walk in total in one week?

Name _____ Class _____ Date _____

MULTIPLE CHOICE

1. Misha has a board that is $17\frac{1}{2}$ inches long that he has to cut into 3 equal pieces. How long should each piece be?

   A. $5\frac{2}{3}$ inches

   B. $5\frac{5}{6}$ inches

   C. $8\frac{3}{4}$ inches

   D. $14\frac{1}{2}$ inches

2. Jenni buys a piece of fabric that is $4\frac{7}{8}$ yards long. What is the decimal equivalent of $4\frac{7}{8}$?

   F. 0.875   H. 4.875

   G. 4.8   J. 4.95

3. A diver is working 30 meters below sea level. Another diver is taking a break on a platform directly above him that is 5 meters above sea level. How far apart are the two divers?

   A. 5 meters   C. 35 meters

   B. 25 meters   D. 40 meters

4. Thuy has $625 in her checking account. She writes two checks for $23 each and then makes one deposit of $146. What is Thuy's final checking account balance?

   F. $433   H. $771

   G. $725   J. $817

5. Uma's salad dressing recipe calls for $\frac{1}{2}$ cup of yogurt. She wants to triple the recipe. How much yogurt does she need?

   A. $1\frac{1}{2}$ cups   C. 3 cups

   B. 2 cups   D. $3\frac{1}{2}$ cups

6. Sally's baked bean recipe calls for 5 pounds of sugar and 20 pounds of dried beans. How many pounds of sugar are needed for a recipe using just 1 pound of dried beans?

   F. $\frac{1}{5}$ pound   H. 1 pound

   G. $\frac{1}{4}$ pound   J. 4 pounds

7. The temperature in Franklin City is −5 °C. The temperature in Silver City is four degrees less. What is the temperature in Silver City?

   A. −9 °C   C. −4 °C

   B. −5 °C   D. 9 °C

8. Jim raised $43.64 for the community food bank. Rina raised $165.23 for the food bank, and Everett raised $23.09 for the food bank. How much did they all raise together?

   F. $66.73   H. $208.87

   G. $165.23   J. $231.96

9. Michel's checking account balance was $345. Michel withdrew $160 three times. What is his current balance?

   A. −$480   C. $135

   B. −$135   D. $185

10. The table below shows Giorgio's scores at a state golf tournament. What is Giorgio's average score for the five rounds?

Round	1	2	3	4	5
Score	3	1	−3	−2	−4

   F. −4   H. −2

   G. −3   J. −1

11. A new poll shows that $\frac{9}{11}$ of all students like to eat pizza. Jan wants to write $\frac{9}{11}$ as a decimal. What is $\frac{9}{11}$ in decimal form?

A. 0.8

B. 0.81

C. 0.8181...

D. 0.90

12. A treasure chest sits 1,256 feet below sea level. A captain looking for the treasure is in a house 769 feet above sea level. What is the vertical distance between the treasure chest and the house?

F. −496 feet

G. 496 feet

H. 1,256 feet

J. 2,025 feet

13. The ABC Corporation had a profit of $3,476 in February. It had a loss of $4,509 in March. What was its net gain for February and March?

A. −$7,985

B. −$1,033

C. $1,033

D. $7,985

FREE RESPONSE

14. Sheila has to pack 128 baskets of apples. She has packed $\frac{1}{4}$ of the baskets. How many baskets are left for her to pack?

_____

_____

_____

15. Marley gets on an elevator on the 30th floor of a building. She goes up 6 floors to pick up a package then goes down 14 floors for a meeting. Write and simplify an expression to show what floor Marley is now on.

_____

_____

_____

16. Leanne was asked on a math test if the number 0.58 is a rational number. She says it is not a rational number. Is she correct? Why or why not?

_____

_____

17. Mr. Frommer's original loan balance was $4,376. He made three monthly payments of $129. He also made an extra payment of $98. Write and simplify an expression that finds Mr. Frommer's new balance.

_____

_____

_____

18. The drop in temperature from 6:00 A.M. to 12:00 P.M. was 14 °F. What is the average hourly drop in temperature for that time frame?

_____

_____

_____

_____

19. Herbert's checking account balance was $233. His account has overdraft protection if he withdraws more than his balance, but the bank charges $12 for covering the overdraft. Herbert made 4 withdrawals of $70 each. Does Herbert's account require overdraft protection? Why or why not? What is his final balance?

_____

_____

_____

_____

_____

Ratios and Proportional Relationships

Unit Focus

You will continue to refine your computation skills as you learn to simplify complex fractions. You'll find unit rates by dividing rational numbers. Proportional relationships are a relationship in which the ratio of one quantity to another is constant. This constant plays an important role in mathematics. You will learn to identify the constant of proportion in tables, graphs, and equations. You'll also be able to recognize when a relationship is not proportional. Finally, you will learn to apply percents to a variety of contexts, including sales tax, commissions, and simple interest.

Unit at a Glance

COMMON CORE

UNIT 2

Unpacking the Common Core State Standards

Use the table to help you understand the Standards for Mathematical Content that are taught in this unit. Refer to the lessons listed after each standard for exploration and practice.

COMMON CORE Standard for Mathematical Content	What It Means For You
CC.7.RP.1 Compute unit rates associated with ratios of fractions, including ratios of lengths, areas and other quantities measured in like or different units. Lesson 2-1	Given two quantities, you will express their relationship as a unit rate. Given a specific quantity, you will use unit rates to find a related quantity. You will simplify complex fractions by dividing.
CC.7.RP.2a Decide whether two quantities are in a proportional relationship, e.g., by testing for equivalent ratios in a table or graphing on a coordinate plane and observing whether the graph is a straight line through the origin. Lesson 2-2, 2-3	You will use the definition of a proportional relationship to determine whether a relationship presented in a table or graph is proportional.
CC.7.RP.2b Identify the constant of proportionality (unit rate) in tables, graphs, equations, diagrams, and verbal descriptions of proportional relationships. Lesson 2-2, 2-3	You will determine the constant of proportionality for proportional relationships. These relationships may be shown in a table, graph, or equation.
CC.7.RP.2c Represent proportional relationships by equations. Lessons 2-2, 2-3	Using the constant of proportionality, you will be able to write an equation that represents a specific proportional relationship.
CC.7.RP.2d Explain what a point (x, y) on the graph of a proportional relationship means in terms of the situation, with special attention to the points $(0, 0)$ and $(1, r)$ where r is the unit rate. Lesson 2-3	Using your understanding of proportional relationships, you will explain how the point $(1, r)$ is related to the unit rate. You'll also explain the meaning of specific points on the graph, such as $(0, 0)$.
CC.7.RP.3 Use proportional relationships to solve multistep ratio and percent problems. Lessons 2-2, 2-3, 2-4	Your understanding of proportional relationships will help you solve problems. You will use your percent skills to solve real-world problems involving simple interest, tax, tips, commissions, fee, percent increase and decrease, and percent error.
CC.7.NS.3 Solve real-world and mathematical problems involving the four operations with rational numbers. Lesson 2-1	You will continue to add, subtract, multiply, and divide with rational numbers; with a specific focus on complex fractions.

Unit Rates

Essential question: *How do you find and compare unit rates?*

COMMON
CORE

CC.7.RP.1
CC.7.NS.3

1 E X P L O R E **Finding Rates**

Jeff hikes $\frac{1}{2}$ mile every $\frac{1}{4}$ hour. Lisa hikes $\frac{1}{3}$ mile every $\frac{1}{6}$ hour. How far do they each hike in 1 hour? 2 hours?

A Use the bar diagram to help you determine how many miles Jeff hikes. How many $\frac{1}{4}$ hours are in 1 hour? How far does Jeff hike in 1 hour?

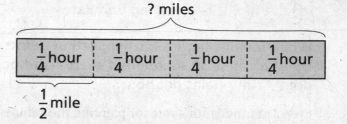

_____

B Complete the table for Jeff's hike.

Distance (mi)	$\frac{1}{2}$				
Time (h)	$\frac{1}{4}$	$\frac{1}{2}$	$\frac{3}{4}$	1	2

C Complete the bar diagram to help you determine how far Lisa hikes. How many miles does she hike in one hour?

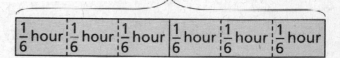

_____

D Complete the table for Lisa's hike.

Distance (mi)	$\frac{1}{3}$				
Time (h)	$\frac{1}{6}$	$\frac{1}{3}$	$\frac{1}{2}$	1	2

REFLECT

1a. How did you find Jeff's distance for $\frac{3}{4}$ hour?

_____

1b. Which hiker walks farther in one hour? What does this tell you about the speeds at which they each hike?

_____

_____

A ratio is used to compare two quantities. When these quantities have different units, the ratio is called a rate. Ratios and rates can be expressed as fractions. When a rate has a denominator of 1, it is called a **unit rate**. To find a unit rate, divide the numerator by the denominator.

Sometimes rates are expressed as complex fractions. A **complex fraction** is a fraction that has a fraction as its numerator, denominator, or both. To simplify a complex fraction, use what you know about dividing rational numbers and divide the fraction in the numerator by the fraction in the denominator.

$$\frac{\frac{a}{b}}{\frac{c}{d}} = \frac{a}{b} \div \frac{c}{d} = \frac{a}{b} \times \frac{d}{c}$$

2 **EXAMPLE** Finding Unit Rates

While remodeling his kitchen, Arthur paints the cabinets. He estimates that he paints 30 square feet every half-hour. How many square feet does Arthur paint per hour?

Step 1: Find Arthur's rate for painting the cabinets.

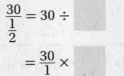

    square feet

    hour

Step 2: Find the unit rate.

$$\frac{30}{\frac{1}{2}} = 30 \div \boxed{}$$ *Rewrite the fraction.*

$$= \frac{30}{1} \times \boxed{}$$ *To divide, multiply by the reciprocal.*

$$= \underline{}$$ *Multiply to find the unit rate.*

Arthur paints _____.

TRY THIS!

2a. Paige mows $\frac{1}{6}$ acre in $\frac{1}{4}$ hour. How many acres does Paige mow per hour?

_____

_____

REFLECT

2b. How could you find the unit rate for **2a** by using a table? Complete the table.

Acres	$\frac{1}{6}$			
Time (h)	$\frac{1}{4}$			

_____

_____

3 EXAMPLE — Comparing Unit Rates

Two containers filled with water are leaking. Container A leaks at a rate of $\frac{2}{3}$ gallon every $\frac{1}{4}$ hour. Container B leaks at a rate of $\frac{3}{4}$ gallon every $\frac{1}{3}$ hour. Determine which container is leaking water more rapidly.

Find the unit rate for container A.

$$\frac{\frac{2}{3}}{\boxed{}} = \frac{2}{3} \boxed{} \boxed{} = \frac{2}{3} \times \boxed{} = \boxed{} = \boxed{} \text{ gallons per hour}$$

Find the unit rate for container B.

$$\frac{\frac{3}{4}}{\boxed{}} = \frac{3}{4} \div \boxed{} = \boxed{} \times \boxed{} = \boxed{} = \boxed{} \text{ gallons per hour}$$

Compare the unit rates.

Compare the whole-number parts of the numbers.

_____ = _____ The whole number parts are equal.

Compare the fractional parts.

Find a common denominator by multiplying the denominators.

_____ × _____ = _____

$$\frac{2}{3} = \frac{\boxed{}}{12} \qquad \frac{1}{4} = \frac{\boxed{}}{12}$$

$\frac{\boxed{}}{12}$ is greater than/less than $\frac{\boxed{}}{12}$.

Therefore, $\boxed{}$ is greater than/less than $\boxed{}$.

Container _____ is leaking more rapidly.

TRY THIS!

3a. Two liquid storage containers are being filled. Liquid enters the first container at a rate of $\frac{2}{3}$ gallon per $\frac{1}{4}$ minute. Liquid pours into the second storage container at a rate of $\frac{3}{5}$ gallon per $\frac{1}{6}$ minute. Determine which container is being filled faster.

_____

_____

_____

REFLECT

3b. How do you know which units to use as the numerator in 3a?

_____

PRACTICE

1. Brandon enters bike races. He bikes $8\frac{1}{2}$ miles every $\frac{1}{2}$ hour. Complete the table to find how far Brandon bikes for each time interval.

Distance (mi)	$8\frac{1}{2}$				
Time (h)	$\frac{1}{2}$	1	$1\frac{1}{2}$	2	$2\frac{1}{2}$

Simplify each complex fraction.

2. $\dfrac{\frac{3}{4}}{\frac{2}{3}} =$ _____

3. $\dfrac{\frac{1}{2}}{\frac{5}{8}} =$ _____

4. $\dfrac{\frac{4}{5}}{\frac{2}{3}} =$ _____

5. $\dfrac{\frac{6}{7}}{\frac{1}{7}} =$ _____

Find each unit rate.

6. Julio walks $3\frac{1}{2}$ miles in $1\frac{1}{4}$ hours.

7. Kenny reads $\frac{5}{8}$ page in $\frac{2}{3}$ minute.

_____

_____

8. Marcia uses $\frac{3}{4}$ cup sugar when she halves the recipe.

9. Sandra tiles $\frac{5}{4}$ square yards in $\frac{1}{3}$ hour.

_____

_____

The information for two cell phone companies is given.

10. What is the unit rate for On Call?

_____

11. What is the unit rate for Talk Time?

_____

On Call	Talk Time
3.5 hours: $10	$\frac{1}{2}$ hour: $1.25

12. Determine which of the companies offers the best deal. Explain your answer.

_____

13. **What if?** Another company offers a rate of $0.05 per minute.

   a. How would you find the unit rate per hour?

   _____

   b. Is this a better deal than On Call or Talk Time?

   _____

Proportional Relationships, Tables, and Equations

COMMON CORE

CC.7.RP.2a
CC.7.RP.2b
CC.7.RP.2c
CC.7.RP.3

Essential question: *How can you use tables and equations to identify and describe proportional relationships?*

1 EXPLORE   **Discovering Proportional Relationships**

A giant tortoise moves at a slow but steady pace. It takes the giant tortoise 3 seconds to travel 10.5 inches.

A Use the bar diagram to help you determine how many inches a tortoise travels in 1 second. What operation did you use to find the answer?

10.5 in.

| 1 sec | 1 sec | 1 sec |

?

_____

B Complete the table.

Time (sec)	1	2	3	4	5
Distance (in.)			10.5		

C For each column of the table, find the ratio of the distance to the time. Write each ratio in simplest form.

$$\frac{Distance}{Time} = \quad \frac{Distance}{Time} = \quad \frac{Distance}{Time} = \quad \frac{Distance}{Time} = \quad \frac{Distance}{Time} = $$

D What do you notice about the ratios? _____

E **Conjecture** How do you think the distance a tortoise travels is related to the time?

_____

REFLECT

1a. Suppose the tortoise travels for 12 seconds. Explain how you could find the distance the tortoise travels.

_____

1b. How would you describe the rate or speed at which a tortoise travels?

_____

A **proportional relationship** is a relationship between two quantities in which the ratio of one quantity to the other quantity is constant. A giant tortoise can live as long as 150 years. One reason these reptiles live so long is their slow heart rate. A giant tortoise's heart beats only 6 times per minute. The giant tortoise's heart rate is an example of a proportional relationship. The ratio of the number of heart beats to the number of minutes is 6.

2 EXAMPLE Identifying Proportional Relationships

Alberto types 45 words per minute. Is the relationship between the number of words and the number of minutes a proportional relationship? Why or why not?

A Complete the table.

Time (min)	1	2	3	4	5
Number of Words	45				

B Complete the ratios.

$$\frac{\text{Number of Words}}{\text{Time}} = \frac{45}{1} = \frac{\;\;\;}{\;\;\;} = \frac{\;\;\;}{\;\;\;} = \frac{\;\;\;}{\;\;\;} = \frac{\;\;\;}{\;\;\;} = \;\;\;$$

The ratios are _____.

The *common ratio* is _____.

So, the relationship is _____.

TRY THIS!

2a. The table shows the distance Allison drove on one day of her vacation. Is the relationship between the distance and the time a proportional relationship? Why or why not?

Time (h)	1	2	3	4	5
Distance (mi)	65	120	195	220	300

REFLECT

2b. Do you think Allison drove at a constant speed for the entire trip? Why or why not?

The equation for a proportional relationship has a special form. If the relationship between x and y is a proportional relationship, then the equation for the relationship may be written as $y = ax$, where a is a positive number. The constant a is called the **constant of proportionality**.

$$y = ax$$

constant of proportionality

3 EXAMPLE Writing an Equation for a Proportional Relationship

Two pounds of cashews cost $5, 3 pounds of cashews cost $7.50, and 8 pounds of cashews cost $20. Show that the relationship between the number of pounds of cashews and the cost is a proportional relationship. Then write an equation for the relationship.

Make a table to find the common ratio. Then write an equation with the common ratio as the constant of proportionality.

A Complete the table.

Number of Pounds	2	3	8
Cost ($)	5		

B Complete the ratios. $\dfrac{\text{Cost}}{\text{Number of Pounds}} = \dfrac{5}{2} = \dfrac{\quad}{\quad} = \dfrac{\quad}{\quad} = \boxed{}$

The common ratio is _____.

C To write an equation, first tell what the variables represent.

Let x represent the number of pounds of cashews.

Let y represent the cost in dollars.

Use the common ratio as the constant of proportionality.

So, the equation for the relationship is _____.

REFLECT

3a. How can you use substitution to check your equation?

_____

3b. What is the unit cost (unit rate) for the cashews? How does the unit cost appear in your equation?

_____

3c. How can you use your equation to find the cost of 6 pounds of cashews?

_____

PRACTICE

Tell whether the relationship is a proportional relationship. If so, give the constant of proportionality.

1.

Number of Minutes	3	4	5	6	7
Number of Seconds	180	240	300	360	420

_____

2.

Time (h)	1	2	3	4	5
Biking Distance (mi)	12	26	36	44	50

_____

3. Naomi reads 9 pages in 27 minutes, 12 pages in 36 minutes, 15 pages in 45 minutes, and 50 pages in 150 minutes.

_____

4. A scuba diver descends at a constant rate of 8 feet per minute.

_____

Write an equation for the relationship. Tell what the variables represent.

5. It takes Li 1 hour to drive 65 miles, 2 hours to drive 130 miles, and 3 hours to drive 195 miles.

_____

_____

6. There are 3.9 milligrams of calcium in each ounce of cooked chicken.

_____

_____

7.

Gallons of Gasoline	3	4	5	6
Total Cost ($)	9.45	12.60	15.75	18.90

_____

_____

8.

Cups of Batter	2	6	8	12
Number of Muffins	5	15	20	30

_____

_____

Information on three car rental companies is given.

9. Write an equation that gives the cost y of renting a car for x days from Rent-All.

_____

10. What is the cost per day of renting a car from A-1?

_____

11. Which company offers the best deal? Why?

_____

Rent-All				
Days	3	4	5	6
Total Cost ($)	55.50	74.00	92.50	111.00

A-1 Rentals	**Car Town**
The cost y of renting a car for x days is given by $y = 22.5x$.	The cost of renting a car from us is just $19.25 per day!

Proportional Relationships and Graphs

COMMON
CORE

CC.7.RP.2a
CC.7.RP.2b
CC.7.RP.2d
CC.7.RP.3

Essential question: *How can you use graphs to represent and analyze proportional relationships?*

1 EXPLORE Graphing Proportional Relationships

Most showerheads that were manufactured before 1994 use 5 gallons of water per minute. Is the relationship between the number of gallons of water and the number of minutes a proportional relationship?

A Complete the table.

Time (min)	1	2	3		10
Water Used (gal)	5			35	

B Based on the table, is this a proportional relationship? Explain your answer.

_____

C Plot the data from the table.

D **Draw Conclusions** If you continued the table to include 23 minutes, would the point (23, 125) be on this graph? Why or why not?

_____

_____

_____

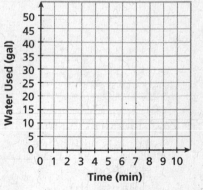

Showerhead Water Use

REFLECT

1a. **What If?** If a line was drawn through the plotted points, does it make sense that it would go through the origin? Explain.

_____

_____

1b. Another showerhead uses less water per minute. How would its graph compare to the one you plotted?

_____

In addition to using a table to determine if a relationship is proportional, you also can use a graph. A relationship is a proportional relationship if its graph is a straight line through the origin.

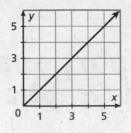

2 EXAMPLE   Identifying Proportional Relationships

An Internet café charges a one-time $5 service fee and then $2 for every hour of use. Is this relationship a proportional relationship?

A   Complete the table.

Time (h)	1	2	5		8
Total Cost ($)	7			17	

B   Plot the data from the table and connect the points with a line.

C   The graph of the data is a _____.

The line does/does not go through the origin.

So, the relationship is _____.

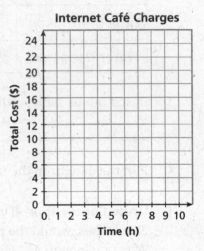

Internet Café Charges

TRY THIS!

2a.   Plot the data from the table and connect the points with a line.

Canoe Rental (h)	2	5	8	10
Total Cost ($)	5	11	17	21

2b.   Is this a proportional relationship? Explain.

_____

_____

_____

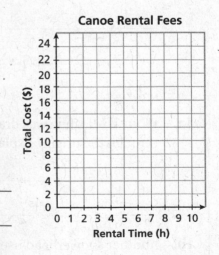

Canoe Rental Fees

You have seen that the equation of a proportional relationship may be written as $y = ax$, where a is a positive number. The constant of proportionality, a, tells you how steep the graph of the relationship is. The greater the value of a, the steeper the line.

3 EXAMPLE Analyzing Graphs

The graph shows the relationship between time in years and the number of centimeters a fingernail grows.

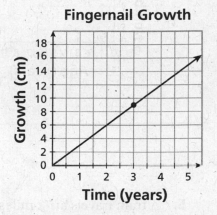

Fingernail Growth

A What does the point (3, 9) represent?

_____

_____

B What is the constant of proportionality? _____

C Write an equation for the relationship. _____

REFLECT

3a. What does the point (0, 0) on the graph represent?

_____

3b. What is the rate at which a fingernail grows? How does this relate to the constant of proportionality?

_____

_____

PRACTICE

Complete each table. Tell whether the relationship is a proportional relationship. Explain why or why not.

1. A student reads 65 pages per hour.

Time (h)	3	5		10
Pages			585	

_____

_____

_____

2. A babysitter makes $7.50 per hour.

Time (h)	2		5	
Earnings		22.50		60

_____

_____

_____

Tell whether the relationship is a proportional relationship. Explain why or why not.

3.

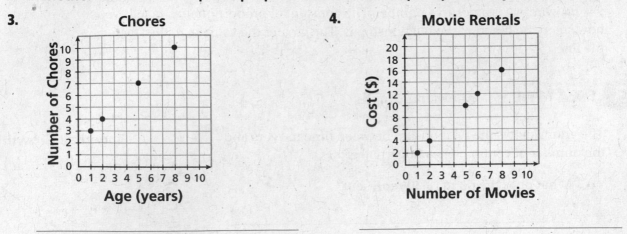

Chores

4. Movie Rentals

_____   _____

_____   _____

_____   _____

5. A train travels at 72 miles per hour. Will the graph of the train's rate of speed show that the relationship between the number of miles traveled and the number of hours is a proportional relationship? Explain.

_____

_____

_____

_____

The graph shows the relationship between time and the distance run by two horses.

6. How long does it take each horse to run 1 mile?

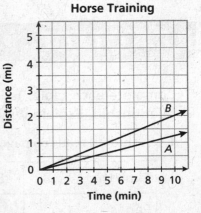

Horse Training

_____

7. What does the point (0, 0) represent?

_____

_____

_____

8. Write an equation for the relationship between time and distance.

_____

9. Draw a line on the graph representing a horse that is faster than each of these.

Applying Percents

Essential question: *How do you use percents to solve problems?*

COMMON
CORE

CC.7.RP.3

1 EXPLORE Finding Total Cost

The bill at a restaurant for the Smith family came to $40. They want to leave a 15% tip. What is the total cost of the meal?

A Find the amount of the tip. Use a bar model.

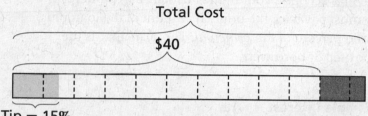

Total Cost

$40

Tip = 15%

The white bar represents $40. It is divided into _____ equal pieces.

Each section represents _____ %, or $ _____.

The tip is 15% or _____ sections of the model.

1 section = $ _____, so $\frac{1}{2}$ of a section = $ _____

$1\frac{1}{2}$ sections = $ _____ + $ _____ = $ _____

The tip is $ _____ .

B Find the total cost of the meal.

To find the total cost of the meal, add together the bill total and the tip.

	+		=	
Bill total		Tip		Total Cost

C Another way to find the tip is to multiply the bill total by the percent of the tip.

Write 15% as a decimal. _____

	×		=	
Bill total		Percent		Tip

	+		=	
Bill total		Tip		Total Cost

1a. How could the Smith family use mental math to calculate the tip?

_____

_____

TRY THIS!

1b. Sharon wants to buy a coat that costs $20. The rate of sales tax is 5%. How much is the sales tax? What is her total cost for the coat?

_____

When you place money in a savings account, your money usually earns interest. When you borrow money, you must pay back the original amount of the loan plus interest. **Simple interest** is a fixed percent of the _principal_. The **principal** is the original amount of money deposited or borrowed.

2 **EXPLORE**   **Finding Simple Interest**

Anita deposits $320 into an account that earns 4% simple interest per year. What is the total amount in the account after 3 years?

A Find the amount of interest earned in one year.
Then calculate the amount of interest for 3 years.

Write 4% as a decimal. _____

Complete the table.

Initial Deposit ($)	×	Interest Rate	=	Interest for 1 year ($)
	×		=	

Interest for 1 year ($)	×		=	Interest for 3 years ($)
	×		=	

B Add the interest for 3 years to the initial deposit to find the total amount in her account after 3 years.

	+		=	
Deposit		Interest		Total

TRY THIS!

2a. **What If?** Anita decides to leave her money in the account. How much will she have in the account after 10 years?

_____

2b. Aaron borrows $400 on a 4-year loan. He is charged 5% simple interest per year. How much interest is he charged in the 4 years? What is the total amount Aaron has to pay back?

_____

2c. **What If?** What if Aaron took out a 6-year loan? How much interest would he have to pay back?

_____

Percents can be used to describe an amount of change. **Percent increase** and **percent decrease** show the amount of change in a value. Percent increase describes how much the original amount increases. Percent decrease describes how much the original amount decreases.

$$\text{percent of change} = \frac{\text{amount of change}}{\text{original amount}}$$

3 EXAMPLE Finding Percent of Change

The price of a pair of shoes increased from $52 to $64. What is the percent increase?

A Find the amount of change.

	−		=	
Greater Value		Lesser Value		Amount of Change

B Find the percent change. Round to the nearest percent.

$$\text{percent of change} = \frac{\text{amount of change}}{\text{original amount}} = \frac{\boxed{}}{52} = \text{\_\_\_\_\_} \times 100 = \text{\_\_\_\_\_}\%$$

TRY THIS!

3a. The number of students at an elementary school in 2001 was 654. In 2007, there were 520 students. What is the percent decrease in the number of students?

_____

REFLECT

3b. Why will the percent of change always be represented by a positive number?

_____

_____

3c. What does a 100% increase mean?

_____

_____

PRACTICE

1. A ticket to a play costs $50. There is a 5% transaction fee. What is the total cost of the ticket?

_____

2. A taxi ride costs $32. Paulie gives the driver a 15% tip. What is the total amount Paulie gives the driver?

_____

3. Emily earns $75 per day plus a commission. Her commission is 15%. She sells $600 worth of furniture. How much does she earn for the day?

_____

4. Martin finds a shirt for $20 at a store. The sign says it is 10% off the original price. Martin must also pay 8.5% sales tax. What is the cost of the shirt before and after the sales tax?

_____

5. Joe borrowed $2,000 from the bank at a rate of 7% simple interest per year. How much interest did he pay in 5 years?

_____

6. You have $550 in a savings account that earns 3% simple interest each year. How much will be in your account in 10 years?

_____

7. **Error Analysis** A store makes a profit of $1,000 in January. In February sales are up 25%, but in March sales are down 25%. The store manager says that the profit for March is still $1,000. What is his error? What is the actual profit for March?

_____

_____

_____

8. Percent error calculations are used to determine how close to the true values, or how accurate, experimental values really are. The formula is similar to finding percent of change.

$$\text{percent error} = \frac{\text{amount of change}}{\text{actual value}} \times 100$$

In chemistry, Bob records the volume of a liquid as 13.3 ml. The actual volume is 13.6 ml. What is his percent error? Round to the nearest percent.

_____

9. Complete the table.

Item	Scooter	Bike
Original Price	$45	$110
New Price	$56	$96
Percent Change		
Increase or Decrease		

UNIT 2

Problem Solving Connections

COMMON CORE

CC.7.RP.1
CC.7.RP.2a, b, c, d
7.RP.3

Car or Motorcycle? The table gives information on the world's fastest car and fastest motorcycle. Suppose the car and motorcycle race for 10 minutes at the rates shown. Which vehicle would win the race (that is, which vehicle would travel farther)? What would be the margin of victory?

World's Fastest Car and Motorcycle			
Vehicle	**Name**	**Time**	**Distance**
Car	SSC Ultimate Aero	$\frac{1}{8}$ min	$\frac{1}{2}$ mi
Motorcycle	Suzuki Hayabusa	$\frac{1}{9}$ min	$\frac{1}{3}$ mi

1 Find Unit Rates

A Find the speed of the car by calculating the unit rate. Show your work below.

B Find the speed of the motorcycle by calculating the unit rate. Show your work below.

C Which vehicle goes faster, the car or the motorcycle? How do you know?

_____

_____

_____

2 Make Tables and Write Equations

A Complete the tables for the car and the motorcycle.

Car					
Time (min)	1	2	3	4	5
Distance (mi)	▢	▢	▢	▢	▢

Motorcycle					
Time (min)	1	2	3	4	5
Distance (mi)	▢	▢	▢	▢	▢

B Are the relationships in the tables proportional relationships? Why or why not?

_____

_____

C What is the constant of proportionality for the car? _____

What is the constant of proportionality for the motorcycle? _____

D How are the constants of proportionality related to the unit rates?

_____

_____

E Write an equation that gives the relationship between time and distance for the car. Tell what the variables represent.

F Write an equation that gives the relationship between time and distance for the motorcycle. Tell what the variables represent.

3 Make Graphs

A Use your tables and/or your equations to graph the relationship for the car and the relationship for the motorcycle. Graph both relationships on the coordinate plane at right.

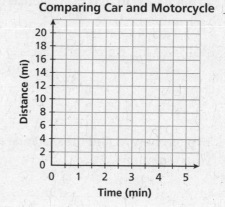

Comparing Car and Motorcycle

Distance (mi) / Time (min)

B How are the two graphs similar?

_____

_____

_____

C How are the two graphs different?

_____

_____

D Do both graphs pass through the origin? Why does this make sense?

_____

_____

E Is it possible to tell which vehicle is faster just by glancing at the graphs? If so, how?

_____

_____

_____

F How can you use the graphs to determine the winner of the race?

_____

_____

_____

4 Answer the Question

A Explain how to find the distance each vehicle travels in 10 minutes using your tables.

_____

_____

_____

B Explain how to find the distance each vehicle travels in 10 minutes using your equations.

_____

_____

C Complete the table to help you find the margin of victory.

Race Summary		
Winner of race (circle one)	Car	Motorcycle
Loser of race (circle one)	Car	Motorcycle
Distance winner travels in 10 minutes		
Distance loser travels in 10 minutes		
Margin of victory		

D **Extend the Ideas** Speeds of cars and motorcycles are most familiar when they are written in miles per hour (mi/h). Use these tables and proportional reasoning to find the speed of each vehicle in miles per hour.

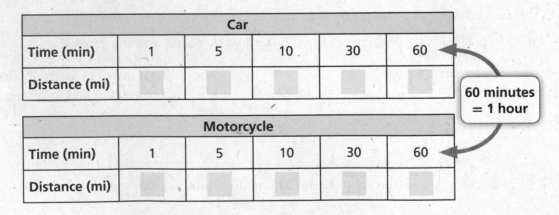

Car					
Time (min)	1	5	10	30	60
Distance (mi)					

Motorcycle					
Time (min)	1	5	10	30	60
Distance (mi)					

60 minutes = 1 hour

Speed of car: _____ mi/h

Speed of motorcycle: _____ mi/h

Name _____ Class _____ Date _____

MULTIPLE CHOICE

1. Lauren jogs at a rate of 2 miles every $\frac{2}{5}$ hour. What is her unit rate?

   A. 0.4 mi/h   **C.** 5 mi/h

   B. 2 mi/h   **D.** 10 mi/h

2. The tables show the number of pages that several students read over a four-day period. Which table shows a proportional relationship?

   F.

Number of Days	1	2	3	4
Total Pages	16	24	32	40

   G.

Number of Days	1	2	3	4
Total Pages	12	24	36	48

   H.

Number of Days	1	2	3	4
Total Pages	15	20	25	30

   J.

Number of Days	1	2	3	4
Total Pages	8	16	27	36

3. An elevator moves at a constant speed of 20 feet per second. Arturo correctly graphs this proportional relationship on a coordinate plane. Which of the following points lies on Arturo's graph?

   A. (0, 20)   **C.** (1, 20)

   B. (20, 0)   **D.** (20, 1)

4. The table below shows a proportional relationship. One of the cells of the table is covered by a drop of ink. What value is covered by the ink?

Time (sec)	3	5	11	17
Distance (ft)	10.2	17	■	57.8

   F. 3.4   **H.** 23

   G. 18.2   **J.** 37.4

5. What is the constant of proportionality for the proportional relationship shown in the graph?

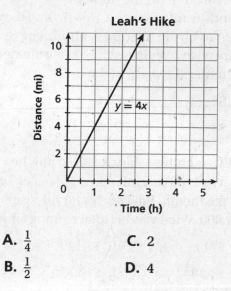

Leah's Hike

$y = 4x$

   A. $\frac{1}{4}$ **C.** 2

   B. $\frac{1}{2}$ **D.** 4

6. Two pounds of dried cranberries cost $5.04, 3 pounds of dried cranberries cost $7.56, and 7 pounds of dried cranberries cost $17.64. Which equation gives the total cost y of x pounds of dried cranberries?

   F. $y = 1.68x$ **H.** $y = 3.04x$

   G. $y = 2.52x$ **J.** $y = 5.04x$

7. Each yard of a fabric costs $4.35. A table shows the number of yards of fabric and the total cost of the fabric. Which of the following must be true about the data in the table?

   A. The ratio of the total cost to the number of yards is always 4.35.

   B. The ratio of the number of yards to the total cost is always 4.35.

   C. The total cost is always 4.35 greater than the number of yards.

   D. The number of yards is always 4.35 times the total cost.

8. The manager of a sporting goods store raises the price of a basketball from $16 to $18. What is the percent increase?

F. 1.25% **H.** 11.1%

G. 2% **J.** 12.5%

9. Three friends have dinner at a restaurant. The total bill for the dinner is $41. The friends want to leave a 15% tip and they want to divide the tip evenly among themselves. Which is the best estimate of each friend's share of the tip?

A. $2 **C.** $4

B. $3 **D.** $6

10. Kalil's monthly salary is $3,250 plus he earns a 1.4% commission on his sales for the month. Kalil's sales for July were $51,000. What was his total earning for July?

F. $714 **H.** $7,140

G. $3,964 **J.** $10,390

FREE RESPONSE

11. A bathtub fills at a constant rate. The amount of water in the tub increases by $\frac{1}{2}$ gallon every $\frac{1}{10}$ minute. What is the unit rate at which the tub fills?

_____

12. In 2000, the population of a town was 50,000. In 2010, the population of the town was 48,000. What is the percent change in the town's population? Is the percent change an increase or a decrease?

_____

13. Explain why a change in price from $20 to $10 is a 50% decrease, but a change in price from $10 to $20 is a 100% increase.

_____

_____

_____

_____

The graph shows the number of servings in different amounts of frozen yogurt. Use the graph for 14 and 15.

Frozen Yogurt

14. Write an equation that gives the number of servings y in x pints of frozen yogurt.

_____

15. Mallory extends the frozen yogurt graph so that it passes through the point $(8, q)$. What is the value of q? What does this point represent?

_____

_____

_____

_____

_____

_____

16. The table shows the amount of money Tyler earns for mowing lawns. Is the relationship a proportional relationship? Why or why not?

Number of Lawns	1	2	3	4
Amount Earned ($)	15	30	48	64

_____

_____

_____

Expressions and Equations

Unit Focus

In this unit you will learn about algebraic expressions, equations, and inequalities. You will learn how to write expressions, equations, and inequalities to represent different real-world scenarios. You will be able to interpret the solutions to these equations and inequalities and adjust the solution sets to make sense in the given scenario. You will be able to determine the rules for when to reverse an inequality symbol when solving an inequality.

Unit at a Glance

COMMON CORE

Unpacking the Common Core State Standards

Use the table to help you understand the Standards for Mathematical Content that are taught in this unit. Refer to the lessons listed after each standard for exploration and practice.

COMMON CORE Standards for Mathematical Content	What It Means For You
CC.7.RP.3 Use proportional relationships to solve multistep ratio and percent problems. Lesson 3-2	You will apply your understanding of proportional relationships to markups and markdowns.
CC.7.EE.1 Apply properties of operations as strategies to add, subtract, factor, and expand linear expressions with rational coefficients. Lesson 3-1	You will combine, multiply, and factor expressions. The Commutative, Associative, and Distributive Properties will help you simplify expressions.
CC.7.EE.2 Understand that rewriting an expression in different forms in a problem context can shed light on the problem and how the quantities in it are related. Lesson 3-2	Given two quantities, you will express their relationship using a unit rate. Given a specific quantity, you will use unit rates to find a related quantity. You will simplify complex fractions.
CC.7.EE.3 Solve multi-step real-life and mathematical problems posed with positive and negative rational numbers in any form (whole numbers, fractions, and decimals), using tools strategically. Apply properties of operations to calculate with numbers in any form; convert between forms as appropriate; and assess the reasonableness of answers using mental computation and estimation strategies. Lesson 3-6	You will decide whether to use expressions, equations, or inequalities when solving problems. Your prior understanding of arithmetic will be combined with your algebraic skills to solve real-life problems.
CC.7.EE.4a Solve word problems leading to equations of the form $px + q = r$ and $p(x + q) = r$, where p, q, and r are specific rational numbers. Solve equations of these forms fluently. Compare an algebraic solution to an arithmetic solution, identifying the sequence of the operations used in each approach. Lesson 3-3	You will solve multi-step equations by identifying the operations involved and undoing them in the opposite order.
CC.7.EE.4b Solve word problems leading to inequalities of the form $px + q > r$ or $px + q < r$, where p, q, and r are specific rational numbers. Graph the solution set of the inequality and interpret it in the context of the problem. Lessons 3-4, 3-5	You will solve one-step and two-step inequalities and graph their solution sets. You'll be able to describe the solution set in the context of a problem.

UNIT 3

Algebraic Expressions

Essential question: *How do you add, subtract, factor, and multiply algebraic expressions?*

COMMON CORE

CC.7.EE.1

1 EXPLORE   Combining Expressions

Jill and Kelly work as consultants and get paid per project. Jill is paid a project fee of $25 plus $10 per hour. Kelly is paid a project fee of $18 plus $14 per hour. Write an expression to represent how much a company will pay to hire both consultants for a project.

A Write expressions for how much Jill and Kelly each make per project.

Jill: $ [ ] + $ [ ] h Kelly: $ [ ] + $ [ ] h

    Fee + Rate per hour   Fee + Rate per hour

B Add both expressions to represent how much the company will pay to hire both consultants.

Let h represent the number of hours they work together.

[ ]   *Combine their pay rates.*

$= 25 + 18 +$ [ ] $+$ [ ]   *Use the Commutative Property.*

$=$ [ ] $+$ [ ] h *Combine like terms.*

The company will pay _____ for both Jill and Kelly to work on their project.

TRY THIS!

1a. How much do Jill and Kelly make individually if they work 10 hours?

_____

1b. Combine $\left(3x + \frac{1}{2}\right) - \left(7x - 4\frac{1}{2}\right)$

$= \left(3x + \frac{1}{2}\right) + \left[\;[\;]\left(7x - 4\frac{1}{2}\right)\right]$ *Subtraction is adding the opposite.*

$= \left(3x + \frac{1}{2}\right) + \left([\;]7x\;[\;]4\frac{1}{2}\right)$ *Distribute the negative sign to each term.*

$= 3x\;[\;]7x + \frac{1}{2}\;[\;]4\frac{1}{2}$ *Use the Commutative Property.*

$=$ [ ]   *Combine like terms.*

1c. What are two different ways to calculate how much a company would pay to hire both Jill and Kelly to work on a 10-hour project?

_____

_____

1d. Explain how the Distributive Property allows you to combine the terms $10h$ and $14h$.

_____

_____

2 **EXPLORE** \ **Using the Distributive Property**

Marc is selling tickets for a concert. Adult tickets cost $16.60, and children's tickets cost $12.20. He gets to keep 25% of the money he collects from ticket sales. Write an expression to represent how much Marc gets to keep.

A Let a represent the number of adult tickets he sells.

Let c represent the number of _____ tickets he sells.

B The expression 16.60 ▢ $+ 12.20$ ▢ represents the _____

_____

C Write 25% as a decimal. _____

D Write an expression to represent 25% of the money he collects.

▢ $\times \left(+ \right)$

25% of adult ticket and children ticket
sales   sales

E Use the Distributive Property to simplify the expression.

$0.25\left(\right) + 0.25\left(\right)$

$= a + c$

TRY THIS!

2. How much does Marc get to keep if he sells 20 adult tickets and 40 children's tickets?

_____

A factor is a number that is being multiplied by another number to get a product. To **factor** is the process of writing a number or an algebraic expression as a product.

3 **EXPLORE**   **Factoring Expressions**

Factor $4x + 8$.

A Model the expression with algebra tiles.

Use _____ positive x tiles and _____ positive one tiles.

B Arrange the tiles to form a rectangle. The total area represents $4x + 8$.

C Since the length multiplied by the width equals area, the length and the width of the rectangle are the factors of $4x + 8$. Find the length and width.

The width is ____ ones tiles, or ____.

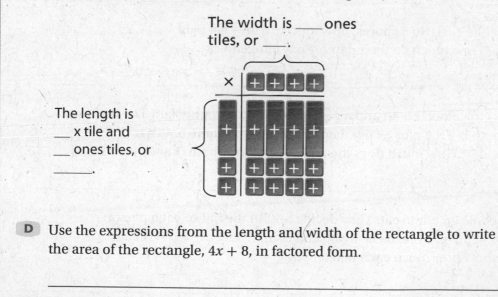

The length is ___ x tile and ___ ones tiles, or _____.

D Use the expressions from the length and width of the rectangle to write the area of the rectangle, $4x + 8$, in factored form.

_____

TRY THIS!

Factor each expression.

3a. $2x + 2$ **3b.** $3x + 9$ **3c.** $5x + 15$ **3d.** $4x + 16$

_____   _____   _____   _____

3e. How could you use the Distributive Property to check your factoring?

_____

3f. **What If?** How would the model and factors change if the original expression was $4x - 8$?

_____

_____

PRACTICE

Add or subtract each expression.

1. $(4.8x + 15.5) + (2.1x - 12.2)$ **2.** $(7x + 8) - (3x + 12)$ **3.** $\left(\frac{1}{2}x + \frac{3}{4}\right) + \left(\frac{1}{2}x - \frac{1}{4}\right)$

_____   _____   _____

4. Each week, Joey gets paid $10 plus $2 for each chore he does. His sister Julie gets paid $5 plus $3 per chore.

  a. Write an expression for how much their parents pay Joey and Julie each week if they do the same amount of chores.

  _____

  b. If Joey and Julie each do 5 chores, how much do they get paid individually? How much do their parents pay altogether?

  _____

5. A company sets up a food booth and a game booth at the county fair. The fee for the food booth is $100 plus $5 per day. The fee for the game booth is $50 plus $7 per day. How much does the company pay for both booths for 5 days?

_____

6. A group of 4 people go out to eat. They decide to split the bill so each person pays $\frac{1}{4}$ of the total price. Appetizers are $6 and main dishes are $9. Write an expression to show how much each person pays.

_____

Factor each expression.

7. $24 + 36x$ **8.** $5x - 25$ **9.** $12x + 10$ **10.** $10x - 60$

_____   _____   _____   _____

3-2

Rewriting Expressions

Essential question: *How can you rewrite expressions to help you solve problems?*

COMMON CORE

CC.7.EE.2
CC.7.RP.3

A percent increase is also known as a markup and a percent decrease is also known as a discount, or markdown.

1 EXPLORE Calculating Markups

To make a profit, a store manager must mark up the prices on the items he sells. A sports store buys skateboards from a supplier for *s* dollars. The store's manager decides to mark up the price for retail sale by 42%.

A   The markup is _____% of the price, *s*.

B   Find the amount of the markup. Use a bar model.

1*s*

0.42*s*

The white bar represents the cost of the skateboard, _____.

The grey section is _____% of _____. This can be written as a decimal, _____.

C   Add _____ to the cost of the skateboard to find the retail price.

Retail price = _____ + _____

                Original cost   Markup

D   You can combine like terms in the expression and write the retail price as a single term.

Retail price = _____

REFLECT

1a.   What are the benefits of writing the price as the sum of two terms? What are the benefits of writing the price as one term?

_____

_____

_____

1b. What If? The markup is changed to 34%; how does the expression for the retail price change?

_____

Keeley is selling bicycles. For the holiday sale, she will mark down each bike's selling price by 24%.

A The markdown is _____% of the price, b.

B Find the amount of the markdown.
Use a bar model.

The white bar represents the cost of the bike, _____.

The grey section is _____% of _____.
This can be written as

a decimal, _____.

C Subtract _____ from the price of the bike to find the sales price.

Sales price = [　　　] − [　　　]

　　　　　Price of bike　　Markdown

D You can combine like terms in the expression and write the sales price as a single term.

Sales price = _____

REFLECT

2a. Conjecture Compare the markup expression from **1** and the markdown expression from **2**. What do you notice about the decimal value in front of the variable for markups and the decimal value in front of the variable for markdowns?

_____

_____

TRY THIS!

1. Rick buys remote control cars to resell. He applies a markup of 10%.
Write two expressions that represent the price of the cars.

_____

2. Jane sells pillows. For a sale she marks them down 5%.

a. Write two expressions that represent the sale price of the pillows. _____

b. If a pillow originally costs $15, what is the sale price? _____

Solving Equations

Essential question: *How do you solve equations that contain multiple operations?*

COMMON CORE

CC.7.EE.4a

1 EXPLORE   Solving Two-Step Equations

Carrie and Freddy collect stamps. Carrie notes that she has twelve less than five times the number of stamps Freddy has. Carrie has 23 stamps. Let *f* be the number of stamps that Freddy has.

A Write an equation that represents Carrie's collection. _____

B Method 1: Solve the equation by covering up the term with the variable.

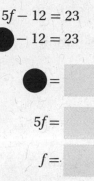

$5f - 12 = 23$

$\bullet - 12 = 23$ Cover the term containing the variable.
Think: "Some number minus 12 equals 23."

$\bullet = \boxed{}$ What number minus 12 equals 23?
Now uncover the term.

$5f = \boxed{}$ *Think*: 5 times some number equals 35.
5 times _____ equals 35.

$f = \boxed{}$

C Method 2: Solve the equation by undoing the operations.
Step 1: Make a table.

First, list the operations in the equation according to the order in which they are applied to the variable.

Operations in the Equation	To Solve
1. First *f* is _____ by 5.	1. First _____ 12 to both sides of the equation.
2. Then, 12 is _____.	2. Then _____ both sides by 5.

Then, starting with the last operation in the equation write the *opposite* of the step. Continue writing the opposite until every step is accounted for.

Step 2: Apply the steps in the "to solve" column to solve the equation.

$5f - 12 = 23$

$5f - 12 \; \boxed{} = 23 \; \boxed{}$

$\dfrac{5f}{\boxed{}} = \dfrac{35}{\boxed{}}$

$f = \boxed{}$

Freddy has _____ stamps.

1a. In what way are these two methods for solving equations similar?

_____

_____

1b. To solve an equation, you isolate the variable by performing _____ operations in the _____ order from the order in which they are applied to the variable in the original equation.

2 **EXPLORE** **Solving Two-Step Equations that Contain Fractions**

Use a table to help you solve each equation.

A $22 = \frac{n}{4} + 7$

Operations in the Equation	To Solve
1. First n is _____ .	**1.** First ____ ____ on both sides of the equation.
2. Then, _____ _____ .	**2.** Then _____ both sides by _____ .

Solution

$22 = \frac{n}{4} + 7$

$22\ \boxed{} = \frac{n}{4} + 7\ \boxed{}$

$15\ \boxed{} = \frac{n}{4}\ \boxed{}$

$\boxed{} = n$

B $\frac{2x}{3} = 12$

Operations in the Equation	To Solve
1. First x is _____ .	**1.** First _____ both sides by _____ .
2. Then, _____ _____ .	**2.** Then _____ both sides by _____ .

Solution

$\frac{2x}{3} = 12$

$\frac{2x}{3}\ \boxed{} = 12\ \boxed{}$

$2x\ \boxed{} = 36\ \boxed{}$

$x = \boxed{}$

TRY THIS!

Solve each equation.

2a. $\frac{x}{3} + 10 = 40$ **2b.** $\frac{x}{2} - 9 = 4$ **2c.** $\frac{2x}{5} = 6$

_____   _____   _____

3 EXAMPLE Solving Equations Using the Distributive Property

Kara used the formula $P = 2(\ell + w)$ to find the perimeter of a photograph. She tells Jim that the length is 6 centimeters and the perimeter is 22 centimeters. How can Jim find the width of the photo?

A Rewrite the formula, substituting the values that you know.

$$\boxed{} = 2\left(\boxed{} + w\right)$$

B Method 1

$$\frac{22}{\boxed{}} = \frac{2(6 + w)}{\boxed{}}$$ Since $(6 + w)$ is being _____ by _____,

_____ by 2 on both sides of the equation.

$$\boxed{} = 6 + w$$ Simplify.

$$11 = 6 + w$$ Then, _____ from both sides.

$$\frac{\boxed{}}{\boxed{}} = \frac{\boxed{}}{}$$

$$\boxed{} = w$$ Simplify.

C Method 2

$$22 = \boxed{}(6) + \boxed{}w$$ Use the Distributive Property.
Distribute _____ to each term in parenthesis.

$$22 = \boxed{} + 2w$$ Simplify.

$$22 = 12 + 2w$$ Then, _____ from both sides.

$$\frac{\boxed{}}{\boxed{}} = \frac{\boxed{}}{\boxed{}}$$

$$\boxed{} = 2w$$ Simplify.

$$\frac{10}{2} = \frac{2w}{2}$$ Now, _____

$$\boxed{} = w$$ Simplify.

TRY THIS!

Solve each equation.

3a. $10 = 4(3 + x)$

_____

3b. $40(x - 2) = 200$

_____

3c. $\frac{1}{2}(2x + 10) = 35$

_____

REFLECT

3d. How are the two solution methods alike?

_____

_____

3e. How are the two solution methods different?

_____

_____

PRACTICE

Solve each equation.

1. $4x + 12 = 60$

_____

2. $5(3x - 4) = 40$

_____

3. $\frac{x}{3} = 33$

_____

4. $\frac{8x}{2} = 24$

_____

5. $2(-3x - 4) = 100$

_____

6. $\frac{-2x}{5} = 2$

_____

7. For 15 weeks, Sue put the same amount of money in a jar. Then she took $9 out to spend on a friend's birthday present. She had $21 left. How much did she put in each week?

_____

8. Matt gives half of his books to the local library and kept the other half. His best friend gives him 3 more books. He now has 57 books. How many did he have to start?

_____

9. Half of Allen's test score plus eight equals 50. What did Allen score on his test?

_____

10. Carl is paid $10 plus $8 an hour. He was paid $66. How many hours did he work?

_____

11. Barry swam three times as many laps as George plus one more lap. Barry swam 25 laps. How many laps did George swim?

_____

12. Gayle has 3 less than two times as many stickers as Robin. Gayle has 25 stickers. How many does Robin have?

_____

13. Mika used the formula $A = \frac{(b_1 + b_2)h}{2}$ to find the area of a trapezoid. Show 2 ways to find the length of the base, b_1, if the area is 32 cm, the height is 4 cm, and the length of b_2 is 6 cm.

$b_1 = $ _____

Solving One-Step Inequalities

Essential question: *How do you solve inequalities that involve one operation?*

COMMON
CORE

CC.7.EE.4b

1 EXPLORE Solving Inequalities

Kate took $3 out of her purse, and she still had at least $8 in it. How much did she have to begin?

The phrases *at least* or *at most* can be confusing. *At least* means that amount or more, so use the greater than or equal to ($\geq$) symbol. *At most* means that amount or less, so use the less than or equal to symbol ($\leq$).

A Write an inequality to represent the amount of money in Kate's purse.

_____

B Use inverse operations to solve the inequality.

$m - 3 \geq 8$ _____ to each side.

$m - 3 \geq \quad 8$ Simplify.

$$\frac{\qquad}{\qquad}$$

$m \geq$ ▢

When graphing an inequality on a number line, use a solid circle to show that the variable can equal that value. Use an empty circle to show that the variable cannot be equal to that value. Since money is not just integer values, you can shade a solid arrow, or ray, to the right.

C Graph the solutions on a number line.

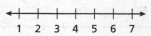

```
0  1  2  3  4  5  6  7  8  9  10 11 12 13 14 15 16 17 18 19 20
```

D What does the solution tell you?

_____

TRY THIS!

Solve. Then graph the solution.

1a. $x + 4 < 9$

```
1  2  3  4  5  6  7
```

_____

REFLECT

1b. Choose a value in the shaded area of the number line from **C** . Substitute it into the original inequality from **A** . Does this value make the inequality true?

_____

1c. Now choose a value outside the shaded area of the number line from C . Substitute it in the original inequality. Does this value make the inequality in A true?

_____

1d. **Conjecture** What does the shaded part of the inequality show?

_____

A value that can be substituted for the variable to make the inequality a true statement is part of the **solution set**. Therefore, 12 is part of the solution set, whereas 10 is not part of the solution set. So, Kate could have had $12 in her purse.

2 EXPLORE   **Inequality Signs**

 A Complete the tables.

Inequality	Multiply each side by:	New Inequality	New Inequality is True or False?
3 < 4	2		
2 ≥ −3	3		
−1 ≤ 6	5		
5 > 2	−1		
1 ≤ 7	−5		
−8 > −10	−8		

Inequality	Divide each side by:	New Inequality	New Inequality is True or False?
4 < 8	4		
12 ≥ −15	3		
−16 ≤ 12	−4		
15 > 5	−5		

 B When both sides of an inequality are multiplied or divided by a _____ number, the inequality is no longer true.

C Complete the tables.

Inequality	Multiply each side by:	New Inequality	Reverse the Inequality Symbol	Reversed symbol makes it True or False?
$5 > 2$	-1	$-5 > -2$		
$1 \le 7$	-5	$-5 \le -35$		
$-8 > -10$	-8	$64 > 80$		

Inequality	Divide each side by:	New Inequality	Reverse the Inequality Symbol	Reversed symbol makes it True or False?
$-16 \le 12$	-4	$4 \le -3$		
$15 > 5$	-5	$-3 > -1$		

REFLECT

2a. Conjecture When both sides of an inequality are multiplied or divided by a negative number, you must _____

to make the statement true.

Properties of Inequalities

- You can add or subtract the same number on both sides of an inequality and the statement will still be true.
- You can multiply or divide both sides of an inequality by the same positive number, and the statement will still be true.
- If you multiply or divide both sides of an inequality by the same negative number, you must reverse the inequality symbol for the statement to still be true.

---

3 EXAMPLE Solving Real-World Inequalities

Michael bought three cans of paint. The bill was less than $60. How much was each can of paint?

A First, write an inequality to represent the situation. Then solve.

$3c < 60$ *Let c represent the cost of the paint.*

$\dfrac{3c}{} \boxed{} \dfrac{60}{}$ *Divide each side by _____.*

$c \boxed{} 20$ *Simplify.*

B What does the solution tell you? Does it make sense for the cost of each paint can to be $0, or less that $0? Explain.

_____

_____

C Graph the solution set.

$-5 \quad 0 \quad 5 \quad 10 \quad 15 \quad 20 \quad 25$

REFLECT

3. Why did you not reverse the inequality sign?

_____

PRACTICE

Solve each inequality.

1. $3x \geq -12$

2. $-4x > 16$

3. $\frac{x}{-2} > -6$

4. $3.5x \leq 14$

_____ _____ _____ _____

5. Karen divided her books onto 6 shelves. There were at least 14 books per shelf. How many books does she have? Write an inequality to represent the situation, then solve.

_____

6. **Error Analysis** A student's solution to the inequality $\frac{x}{-9} > 5$ was $x > -45$. What error did the student make in the solution?

_____

7. Lina bought 4 smoothies at a health food store. The bill was less than $16.

a. Write and solve an inequality to represent the cost of each smoothie.

_____

b. Is the graph of the solution set a solid ray or individual points? Explain.

_____

_____

c. Does it make sense for the cost of each smoothie to be $0 or less than $0? Explain.

_____

_____

d. Graph the solution set.

$-1 \quad 0 \quad 1 \quad 2 \quad 3 \quad 4 \quad 5$

Solving Two-Step Inequalities

Essential question: *How do you solve inequalities that involve multiple operations?*

1 EXPLORE Solving Two-Step Inequalities

As a salesperson, you are paid $52 per week plus $3 per sale. This week you want your pay to be at least $100. Write an inequality for the number of sales you need to make, and describe the solutions.

A Write an inequality to represent the number of sales you need in order to be paid at least $100 for the week.

_____

B Method 1: Solve the equation by covering up the term with the variable.

$3x + 52 \geq 100$

● $+ 52 \geq 100$ Cover the term containing the variable.
     Think: "Some number plus 52 is at least 100."
● $\geq$ ☐   What number plus 52 is at least 100?
     Now uncover the term.

$3x \geq$ ☐   *Think:* 3 times some number is at least 48.

$x \geq$ ☐   3 times _____ equals 48.

C Method 2: Solve the equation by undoing the operations.
Step 1: Make a table.

First, list the operations in the inequality according to the order in which they are applied to the variable

Operations in the Inequality	To Solve
1. First x is _____ by 3.	**1.** First _____ 52 from both sides of the equation.
2. Then, 52 is _____.	**2.** Then _____ both sides by 3.

Then, starting with the last operation in the inequality write the *opposite* of the step. Continue writing the opposite until every step is accounted for.

Step 2: Apply the steps in the "to solve" column to solve the inequality.

$3x + 52 \geq 100$

$3x + 52 \geq 100$

$$\frac{3x}{☐} \geq \frac{48}{☐}$$

$x \geq$ ☐

You must make at least _____ sales.

1a. How can you check your solution?

_____

_____

1b. Would the graph of the solution set be a ray or individual points? Explain your answer.

_____

_____

2 **EXAMPLE** **Solving Two-Step Inequalities Containing Fractions**

Solve $\frac{x}{-4} - 5 < -2$. Then graph the solution set.

A Complete the table and solution steps.

Operations in the Inequality	To Solve	Solution $\frac{x}{-4} - 5 < -2$
1. First x is _____.	**1.** First _____ to both sides of the inequality.	$\frac{x}{4} - 5 < -2$
2. Then, _____ _____.	**2.** Then _____ both sides by _____ and reverse the inequality symbol.	$\frac{x}{-4}(-4) \quad 3(-4)$ $x > \quad$

B Graph the solution on a number line. Put an _____ circle on -12, since the inequality sign is greater than, not greater than or equal to. Then, the ray goes to the _____.

$$\xleftarrow{\qquad}\; | \quad | \quad | \quad | \quad | \quad | \quad |\; \xrightarrow{\qquad}$$
$$-14 \quad -13 \quad -12 \quad -11 \quad -10 \quad -9 \quad -8$$

TRY THIS!

Solve each inequality.

2a. $-13 > \frac{x}{8} - 3$ **2b.** $40 \leq -3x + 10$ **2c.** $-\frac{x}{3} + 5 < -10$

_____   _____   _____

REFLECT

2d. How is solving inequalities different from solving equations?

_____

_____

3 **E X A M P L E** Solving Real-World Inequalities

Cathy has $100 saved to spend on clothes. She wants to purchase a winter jacket for $40 and some sweaters that cost $20 each. How many sweaters can Cathy buy?

A Write an inequality that represents the situation.

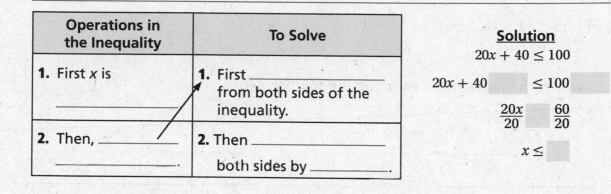

Operations in the Inequality	To Solve	Solution
1. First x is _____	**1.** First _____ from both sides of the inequality.	$20x + 40 \leq 100$
2. Then, _____ _____.	**2.** Then _____ both sides by _____.	$20x + 40 \quad \leq 100$ $\dfrac{20x}{20} \quad \dfrac{60}{20}$ $x \leq$

Cathy can buy _____ sweaters.

Since it is / is not possible to buy a negative number of sweaters, a graph of the solution set will / will not include values less than 0. Cathy could not have bought part of a sweater so the graph is a _____.

B Graph the solution set.

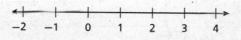

TRY THIS!

3a. A CD costs $12 and a DVD costs $15. You have $60. You plan to buy 1 DVD and some CDs. Write and solve an inequality to determine how many CDs you can buy. What does the solution mean in this situation?

_____

_____

REFLECT

3b. Would you use a ray or a set of points for this solution? What is the solution set? Explain.

_____

_____

_____

PRACTICE

Solve each inequality. Round to the nearest hundredth, if necessary.

1. $10x + 4 \geq -6$

2. $-3x - 21 > 16$

3. $\frac{x}{2} + 1 \geq 4\frac{1}{2}$

_____

_____

_____

4. $\frac{x}{-5} + 11 < 15$

5. $1.5x - 2 \leq 16$

6. $0.2 > -1.2x - 5.1$

_____

_____

_____

Solve each inequality. Then graph the solution set.

7. $-5x - 17 \leq 38$

8. $42 < -\frac{y}{9} + 30$

_____

_____

```
<-+--+--+--+--+--+--+--+--+--+--+-->
 -12 -11 -10 -9 -8 -7 -6 -5 -4 -3 -2 -1  0
```

```
<-+--+--+--+--+--+--+-->
 -113 -112 -111 -110 -109 -108 -107
```

9. Dominique has $5.00. Bagels cost $0.60 each and a small container of cream cheese costs $1.50.

a. How many bagels can Dominique buy if she also buys one small container of cream cheese? Explain your answer.

_____

_____

_____

b. Graph the solution set.

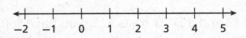

```
<-+--+--+--+--+--+--+--+-->
 -2 -1  0  1  2  3  4  5
```

Yasmine and Alex each have $200 to spend on clothes. Use the table for 10–11.

10. Yasmine decides to purchase a jacket and some long-sleeve shirts. How many long-sleeve shirts can she buy?

Item	Price ($)
Short-sleeve shirt	15
Long-sleeve shirt	20
Pair of jeans	30
Jacket	50

_____

11. Alex wants to buy a jacket, 2 long-sleeve shirts, and some short-sleeve shirts. Can she buy at least 8 short-sleeve shirts? Explain.

_____

_____

3-6

Solving Problems with Expressions, Equations, and Inequalities

COMMON CORE

CC.7.EE.3

Essential question: *How can you solve problems by using expressions, equations, and inequalities?*

1 **EXPLORE** **Solving Problems Using Expressions**

At the beginning of the year, a stock was worth $41. By the end of the year, its value had increased 18.9%.

A Estimate the value of the stock at the end of the year. Use a bar model.

Round 41 to ▢ and 18.9 to 20. As a fraction, 20% is written as ▢ .

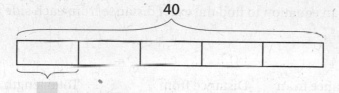

The white bar represents $40. It is divided into _____ equal pieces.

Each section represents _____, or $_____.

The value of the stock increases by an amount represented by 1 section of the model, so add 1 section to the end of the bar to find the stock's end-of-year value.

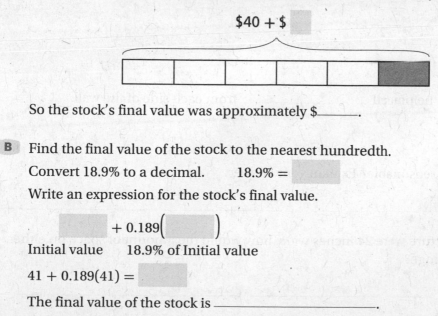

$40 + $▢

So the stock's final value was approximately $_____.

B Find the final value of the stock to the nearest hundredth.

Convert 18.9% to a decimal.   18.9% = ▢

Write an expression for the stock's final value.

$$ \boxed{} + 0.189\left(\boxed{} \right) $$

Initial value   18.9% of Initial value

$$ 41 + 0.189(41) = \boxed{} $$

The final value of the stock is _____.

1a. Was your estimate reasonable? Explain.

_____

1b. Recall that the final retail value of a markup could be written as a single term. What is a single term that can be used to find the exact value of the stock?

_____

2 **EXPLORE** Solving Problems Using Equations

Carl is hanging a picture, and he wants to center it on the wall. The picture is $18\frac{1}{2}$ inches long, and the wall is $60\frac{3}{4}$ inches long.

$60\frac{3}{4}$ inches

x inches   _____ x inches

$18\frac{1}{2}$ inches

A Estimate how many inches from each side of the wall the picture should be placed. _____

B Use the diagram to write an equation to find the exact distance from each side the picture needs to be placed.

[ ] = [ ] + [ ] + [ ]

Total length   Distance from   Distance from   Total length
of wall   side of wall   side of wall   of picture

Combine like terms and solve the equation for the variable.

$60\frac{3}{4}$ = [ ] + [ ]

$$\frac{[\quad]}{2} = \frac{[\quad]}{2}$$

[ ] = [ ]

C The picture should be placed _____ from each side of the wall.

2a. Was your estimate reasonable? Explain your answer.

_____

2b. **What If?** If the picture were 24 inches wide, how would the amount of space on either side of the wall change?

_____

A town has a population of 53,000. The mayor wants to know what percent increase would be necessary for the town's population to be greater than 55,000.

A Write an inequality that represents the situation.

[ ] + [ ] > [ ]

Current population   Increase in population   Target population

B The population needs to increase by 2,000. Estimate what percent 2,000 is of the current population, 53,000. _____

C Use your graphing calculator to help you estimate the percent increase. Enter the expression on the left side of your inequality for Y_1. Set your table to start at 0, and have a step value of 0.01, or 1%.

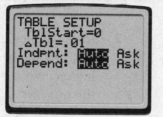

```
TABLE SETUP
 TblStart=0
 ΔTbl=.01
Indpnt: Auto Ask
Depend: Auto Ask
```

D Use a table to see the population at various percent increases. Find where the population is greater than 55,000.

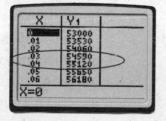

```
 X    │ Y₁
 0    │ 53000
 .01  │ 53530
 .02  │ 54060
 .03  │ 54590
 .04  │ 55120
 .05  │ 55650
 .06  │ 56180
X=0
```

A percent increase between _____% and _____% will make the population reach 55,000.

E Now find the percentage by solving the inequality from **A** . Round your answer to the nearest thousandth if necessary.

$$53,000 + 53,000x > 55,000$$

$$53,000 + 53,000x > 55,000$$

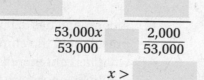

$$\frac{53,000x}{53,000} \quad \frac{2,000}{53,000}$$

$$x > \boxed{}$$

Write the decimal as a percent. _____

A percent increase greater than _____% will increase the population to more than 55,000.

3a. How could the table be used to get a better estimate?

_____

_____

3b. Did you get an exact answer by solving the inequality?

_____

_____

PRACTICE

1. Mary got $\frac{8}{10}$ questions right on her test. With what percentage increase could her test have been at least a 90?

2. Joe's balance in his checking account is $132. At the end of the month, it is 15.3% higher. What is his balance at the end of the month?

3. Diane is centering a $3\frac{1}{2}$-inch-long picture on a 12-inch-wide scrapbook page. How far from the side edges should she put the picture?

4. The quarterback was sacked x yards from his own goal as the first quarter ended. He walked to the other end of the field and lined up on the other x yard line. He walked $41\frac{3}{4}$ yards between the two yard lines. How far from his end zone was he sacked?

5. Last year, Mr. Jones made $30,000. His boss just informed him that he will be receiving at least an 11.2% raise for this year. How much will he make this year?

6. In March, a share of stock was worth $55. Six months later the value of the stock decreased by 7.2%. Find the final value of the stock.

7. There were 348 students in the school last year. The school expects a 7.25% increase in enrollment this year. How many students do they expect to be in the school this year?

8. A company has 350 workers. The president of the company wants to know what percent increase in employment would be necessary for the number of workers to be greater than 375.

UNIT 3

Problem Solving Connections

COMMON CORE

CC.7.EE.1, CC.7.EE.2,
CC.7.EE.3,
CC.7.EE.4a, b,
CC.7.RP.3

To Buy or Not To Buy? *Beau and Belle* and *Fine and Fancy* sell formal attire to the students at Wallace High School. Charlene has been looking at one dress in particular. She hears that both stores will be having a big sale. Will she be able to purchase the dress with her $65 budget limit?

Formal Wear Stores

Store	Percent Markup
Beau and Belle	35
Fine and Fancy	47

1 Write and Evaluate Expressions

A Write an expression that represents the cost of the dress after the markup at *Beau and Belle*.

_____

B *Beau and Belle* buys the dress Charlene wants at a wholesale market for $55. What price will they charge their customers? Show your work below.

C Write an expression that represents the cost of the dress after the markup at *Fine and Fancy*.

_____

D *Fine and Fancy* buys the same dress at another wholesale market for $48. What price will they charge their customers? Show your work below.

E At which retail store is the price less expensive? _____

2 Write and Solve Equations

Charlene asks each store to give her the total price she would have to pay after sales tax.

Formal Wear Stores	
Store	Total Price ($)
Beau and Belle	76.48
Fine and Fancy	76.91

A How does sales tax impact the price of the dress?

_____

B Write an equation that could be used to determine the amount of sales tax charged at *Beau and Belle*. _____

C Find the sales tax rate. Show your work below.

D Write an equation that could be used to determine the amount of sales tax charged at *Fine and Fancy*. _____

E Find the sales tax rate. Show your work below.

F Charlene is looking at a pair of earrings that costs $10. Find the total cost of the earrings if there is a 15% discount and the sales tax is 8%. Does it matter if the discount is taken before or after the sales tax is added? Show your work below.

3 Write and Solve Inequalities

A Write an inequality that can be used to calculate how much of a markdown *Beau and Belle* must take for Charlene to stay within her budget.

_____

B Find the percent markdown Charlene hopes for at *Beau and Belle*.

_____

C Write an inequality that calculates how much of a markdown *Fine and Fancy* must take for Charlene to stay within her budget.

_____

D Find the percent markdown she hopes for at *Fine and Fancy*.

_____

E *Beau and Belle* has a sale with a 12% discount.
Find the final price of the dress after the discount. _____

F Is the 12% discount enough? Explain using the answer to **B** .

_____

_____

_____

G *Fine and Fancy* has a sale with a 15.5% discount.
Find the final price of the dress after the discount. _____

H Is the 15.5% discount enough to make the dress fit within Charlene's budget? Explain using the answer to **D** .

_____

_____

_____

4 Answer the Question

A Explain how Charlene will know if she can buy the dress.

_____

_____

_____

B Both stores advertise a special 20% off sale. Write two expressions that represent the price after a 20% markdown.

_____

C Complete the table to help you find the final price at each store.

Store	Cost	Markup	Retail Price	Special Sale Markdown	Sale Price	Sales Tax	Final Price
Beau and Belle	$55			20%			
Fine and Fancy	$48			20%			

D What store has the best price for Charlene?

_____

E If Charlene wants to purchase her dress and the earrings she looked at on sale, is she able to do so on her budget?

_____

_____

F Charlene's mother says she will give her a $10 loan at a simple interest rate of 2%. Complete the table to find the amount of interest Charlene pays in 1 month.

Loan ($)	×	Interest Rate	=	Interest for a Month
10	×		=	

G What is the total amount Charlene will have to pay her mother back if she pays off the loan in 1 month? 3 months?

_____

H Describe some reasons why Charlene might choose to buy the dress at one store over the other.

_____

_____

_____

Name _____ Class _____ Date _____

MULTIPLE CHOICE

1. Maya has read two less than four times the number of books Theo has read. What factored expression represents the number of books, x, Maya has read?

   A. $4x - 2$ **C.** $2(x - 1)$

   B. $4(x - 2)$ **D.** $2(2x - 1)$

2. Hannah has $175 to spend. She buys $120 worth of non-taxable items. Some other items are taxable at 6%. Which inequality shows how much she can spend on taxable items before tax is applied?

   F. $x \leq \$3.30$ **H.** $x \leq \$51.89$

   G. $x \leq \$45.09$ **J.** $x \leq \$165.09$

3. Let p represent the price of a shirt. Joe has to pay sales tax of 10%. Which expression represents the total amount that Joe pays?

   A. p **C.** $10p$

   B. $1.1p$ **D.** $p + 10$

4. A mover notes the weights of a table and 4 chairs and records $t + 4c \geq 100$ on his invoice. What is he communicating?

   F. The table and 4 chairs each weigh more than 100 pounds.

   G. The table and 4 chairs weigh at most 100 pounds.

   H. The table and 4 chairs weigh around 100 pounds, give or take a little.

   J. The table and 4 chairs weigh at least 100 pounds.

5. Martha buys tennis rackets for $45 dollars. She marks them up 25% before selling them. What is the retail price of the tennis racket?

   A. $11.25   **C.** $56.25

   B. $54.00   **D.** $112.50

6. Brad bought a skateboard for $2 less than half its original price. If he paid $21.50, which skateboard did he buy?

Skateboard	Price ($)
Go Green	45
Speedster	47
Up and Down	43
With the Flow	41

   F. Go Green   **H.** Up and Down

   G. Speedster   **J.** With the Flow

7. Eric sells movie tickets. Adult tickets cost $8 and children's tickets cost $5. He keeps 15% of his sales. Which expression represents how much he keeps?

   A. $1.2a + 0.75c$ **C.** $15(8a + 5c)$

   B. $8a + 5c$ **D.** $0.15(13ac)$

8. Ken has $18 to spend on two models of the solar system and supplies to paint them. The two models cost the same amount. His paint supplies cost $4.62. Which expression indicates how much he can spend on each model?

   F. $x \leq \$6.69$ **H.** $x \leq \$13.38$

   G. $x \geq \$6.69$ **J.** $x \geq \$13.38$

9. Mrs. Hughes' class has 22 students. Her principal tells her that her class will increase to 30 students. Which equation can be used to find the percent increase?

   A. $22 + x = 30$ **C.** $22 + 22x = 30$

   B. $22 = 30x$ **D.** $30 - 22x = x$

10. Which inequality can be used to find how many $1.25 snack packs can be purchased for $10.00?

   F. $1.25s \geq 10.00$ **H.** $\frac{s}{1.25} \geq 10.00$

   G. $1.25s \leq 10.00$ **J.** $\frac{s}{1.25} \leq 10.00$

11. The price of mailing a small package is $0.32 for the first ounce and $0.21 for each additional ounce. Sandra paid $1.16 to mail her package. How much did it weigh?

A. 4 ounces   **C.** 6 ounces

B. 5 ounces   **D.** 7 ounces

12. A bench is being centered on a wall. The wall is 2.7 m long and the bench is 1.8 m wide. Which equation can be used to determine how much of the wall should be on each side of the bench?

F. $2.7 - 1.8x = 2$

G. $1.8x - 2 = 2.7$

H. $2x - 1.8 = 2.7$

J. $2.7 - 2x = 1.8$

13. Shawn sells sunglasses for s dollars. For his winter sale, he marks them down by 33%. Which expression represents the sale price of the sunglasses?

A. $0.33s$ **C.** $0.67s$

B. $0.66s$ **D.** $1.33s$

FREE RESPONSE

14. Henry is putting a new baseboard around his room. He used the formula $P = 2(\ell + w)$ to find the perimeter. The perimeter is $72\frac{1}{2}$ feet. He remembers that the width was $16\frac{1}{2}$ feet. Show two different ways to find the length of the other wall.

_____

_____

_____

_____

15. A baseball stadium has seats in the three areas listed in the table.

Type of Seat	Number of Seats
Lower Deck	10,238
Upper Deck	26,142
Box level	721

Suppose all the box level seats during a game are filled. Write and solve an inequality to determine how many people could be sitting in the other seats.

_____

_____

_____

16. Katia has one more than five times the number of wristbands that Shelly has. Rae has three more than twice the number that Shelly has. What expression would show how many more wristbands Katia has than Rae? Show your work.

_____

_____

_____

_____

17. Lacey has $20 to spend on school supplies. Notebooks cost $2.50, pens cost $0.50 and pencils cost $0.12. Lacey needs 7 notebooks for her classes and also wants to get 4 pens. How many pencils cans she buy? Explain.

_____

_____

_____

_____

Geometry: Modeling Geometric Figures

Unit Focus

In this unit, you will learn about scale drawings and scales. You will learn how to find dimensions for actual objects using the scale. You will learn about conditions that always result in unique triangles and conditions that do not always result in unique triangles. You will identify the figures formed by cross sections of three-dimensional objects. You will identify different types of angle pairs and solve simple equations to find unknown angle measures in a figure.

Unit at a Glance

COMMON
CORE

UNIT 4

Unpacking the Common Core State Standards

Use the table to help you understand the Standards for Mathematical Content that are taught in this unit. Refer to the lessons listed after each standard for exploration and practice.

COMMON CORE **Standards for Mathematical Content**	**What It Means For You**
CC.7.G.1 Solve problems involving scale drawings of geometric figures, including computing actual lengths and areas from a scale drawing and reproducing a scale drawing at a different scale. Lesson 4-1	You will learn how to calculate actual measurements from a scale drawing. You will draw geometric figures at different scales.
CC.7.G.2 Draw (freehand, with ruler and protractor, and with technology) geometric shapes with given conditions. Focus on constructing triangles from three measures of angles or sides, noticing when the conditions determine a unique triangle, more than one triangle, or no triangle. Lesson 4-2	You will draw triangles given certain sets of conditions, such as the measures of two angles and the included side, the lengths of all three sides, or the lengths of two sides and the measure of the angle that is not included between the two sides.
CC.7.G.3 Describe the two-dimensional figures that result from slicing three-dimensional figures, as in plane sections of right rectangular prisms and right rectangular pyramids. Lesson 4-3	You will identify the figures formed by cross sections. You will also sketch cross sections of three-dimensional figures.
CC.7.G.5 Use facts about supplementary, complementary, vertical, and adjacent angles in a multi-step problem to write and solve simple equations for an unknown angle in a figure. Lesson 4-4	You will learn about supplementary, complementary, vertical, and adjacent angles. You will solve simple equations to find the measure of an unknown angle in a figure.

Scale Drawings

Essential question: *How can you use scale drawings to solve problems?*

1 **EXPLORE** Finding Dimensions

A blueprint is a technical drawing
that usually displays architectural
plans. Pete's blueprint shows a layout
of a house. Every 4 inches in the
blueprint represents 3 feet of the
actual house. One of the walls in the
blueprint is 24 inches long. What is
the actual length of the wall?

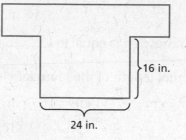

16 in.

24 in.

A Complete the table to find the actual length of the wall.

Blueprint length (in.)	4	8	12	16	20	24
Actual length (ft)	3	6				

TRY THIS!

1a. In Pete's blueprint the length of a side
wall is 16 inches. Find the actual length
of the wall.

_____

1b. The back wall of the house is 33 feet
long. What is the length of the back wall
in the blueprint?

_____

REFLECT

1c. How do you know your answer to **1b** is reasonable?

_____

_____

_____

A **scale drawing** is a proportional two-dimensional drawing of an object. Scale
drawings can represent objects that are smaller or larger than the actual object.

A **scale** is a ratio between 2 sets of measurements. It shows how a dimension
in a scale drawing is related to the actual object. Scales are usually shown as
two numbers separated by a colon such as 1:20 or 1 cm:1 m. Scales can be shown
in the same unit or in different units.

You can solve scale-drawing problems by using proportional reasoning.

2 EXAMPLE   Using a Scale Drawing to Find Area

The figure at the right is a scale drawing of a large rectangular room. What is the area of the actual room?

Set up proportions to help you solve the problem.

10 cm

7 cm

2 cm:5 m

A Find the number of meters represented by 1 cm in the drawing.

$$\frac{2 \text{ cm}}{5 \text{ m}} \overset{\div 2}{=} \frac{1 \text{ cm}}{? \text{ m}} \Rightarrow \frac{2 \text{ cm}}{5 \text{ m}} = \frac{1 \text{ cm}}{\boxed{} \text{ m}}$$

1 cm in this drawing is equal to _____ m in the actual room.

B Find the actual length of the room labeled 7 cm in the drawing.

$$\frac{1 \text{ cm}}{2.5 \text{ m}} \overset{\times 7}{=} \frac{7 \text{ cm}}{? \text{ m}} \Rightarrow \frac{1 \text{ cm}}{2.5 \text{ m}} = \frac{7 \text{ cm}}{\boxed{} \text{ m}}$$

The length of the side labeled 7 cm represents _____ m.

C Find the actual length of the room labeled 10 cm in the drawing.

$$\frac{1 \text{ cm}}{2.5 \text{ m}} = \frac{\boxed{} \text{ cm}}{? \text{ m}} \Rightarrow \frac{1 \text{ cm}}{2.5 \text{ m}} = \frac{\boxed{} \text{ cm}}{\boxed{} \text{ m}}$$

The length of the side labeled 10 cm represents _____ m.

D Since area is length times width, the area of the actual room is

_____ m × _____ m = _____ m².

TRY THIS!

2a. Find the length and width of the actual room, then find the area of the actual room. Round your answer to the nearest tenth.

_____

_____

_____

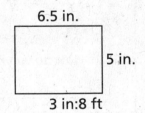

6.5 in.

5 in.

3 in:8 ft

REFLECT

2b. How could you solve **2** without having to determine the number of meters represented by 1 cm?

_____

_____

_____

_____

EXPLORE   **Drawing in Different Scales**

A   In the scale drawing, assume the rectangle is drawn on centimeter grid paper. The scale is 1 cm:3 m.

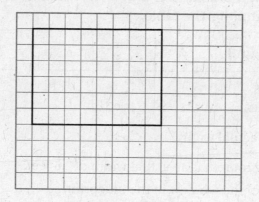

Suppose you redraw the rectangle on centimeter grid paper using a scale of 1 cm:6 m. In the new scale, 1 cm represents more than / less than 1 cm in the old scale.

The measurement of each side of the new rectangle will be twice / half as long as the measurement of the original rectangle.

B   Draw the rectangle for the new scale 1 cm:6 m.

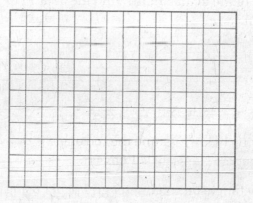

REFLECT

3a.   Find the actual length of each side of your original drawing using the old scale, 1 cm:3 m. Find the actual length of each side of your new drawing using the new scale. How do you know your answers are correct?

_____

_____

_____

_____

The scale of a room in a blueprint is 3 in:5 ft. A wall in the same blueprint is 18 in. Complete the table.

Blueprint length (in.)	3					
Actual length (ft)						

a. How long is the actual wall? _____

b. A window in the room has an actual width of 2.5 feet.
Find the width of the window in the blueprint. _____

2. The scale in the drawing is 2 in.:4 ft. What are the length and width of the actual room? Find the area of the actual room.

_____

_____ 7 in.

14 in.

3. The scale in the drawing is 2 cm:5 m. What are the length and width of the actual room? Find the area of the actual room.

_____

_____

_____ 6 cm

10 cm

4. In the scale drawing below, assume the rectangle is drawn on centimeter grid paper. The scale is 1 cm:4 m.

a. Redraw the rectangle on centimeter grid paper using a scale of 1 cm:6 m.

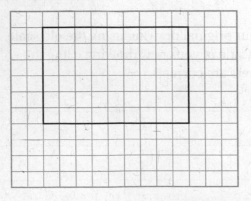 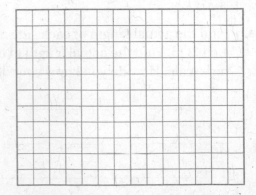

b. What is the actual length and width of the rectangle using the original scale? What are the actual dimensions using the new scale?

_____

Geometric Drawings

Essential question: *How can you draw shapes that satisfy given conditions?*

COMMON
CORE

CC.7.G.2

1 EXPLORE Two Angles and Their Included Side

Draw each triangle with the given conditions.

Triangle 1	Triangle 2
Angles: 30° and 80°	Angles: 55° and 50°
Included side: 2 inches	Included side: 1 inch

Use a ruler and a protractor to draw each triangle with the given angles and included side length.

A Draw Triangle 1.

Step 1: Use a ruler to draw a line that is 2 inches long. This will be the included side.

Step 2: Place the center of the protractor on the left end of the 2-in. line. Then make a 30°-angle mark.

Step 3: Draw a line connecting the left side of the 2-in. line and the 30°-angle mark. This will be the 30° angle.

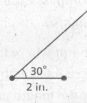

Step 4: Repeat Step 2 on the right side of the triangle to construct the 80° angle.

Step 5: The side of the 80° angle and the side of the 30° angle will intersect. This is Triangle 1 with angles of 30° and 80° and an included side of 2 inches.

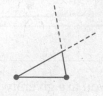

B Draw Triangle 2.

1a. **Conjecture** When you are given two angle measures and the length of the included side, do you get a unique triangle?

_____

_____

2 EXPLORE Two Sides and a Non-Included Angle

Use a ruler, protractor, and compass to construct a triangle with given lengths of 2 inches and $1\frac{1}{2}$ inches and a non-included angle of 45°. A non-included angle is the angle not between the two given sides.

Step 1: Use a ruler to draw a straight line. This will be part of the triangle, but does not have to measure a specific length.

Step 2: As in ❶ , place the center of the protractor on the left end of the line. Then make a mark at the correct 45-degree point. Use your ruler to make this side of the triangle 2 inches long.

Step 3: Make your compass the width of $1\frac{1}{2}$ inches. Place the sharp point on the end of the 2-inch side that you just drew in **Step 2**. Rotate the compass until it intersects, or meets, the bottom line twice (see figure).

Step 4: The point where the compass crosses the bottom line shows where a line can be drawn that is exactly $1\frac{1}{2}$ inches long. Use your ruler to verify the length and draw the line.

2a. Is there another triangle that can be drawn with the given conditions?

_____

_____

2b. When you are given two side lengths and the measure of a non-included angle, do you get a unique triangle? Explain.

_____

_____

_____

_____

Use geometry software to draw a triangle whose sides
have the following lengths: 2 units, 3 units, and 4 units.

Step 1: Draw three line segments of 2, 3, and 4 units
of length.

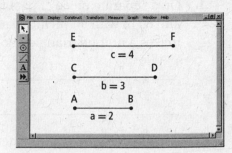

Step 2: Let $\overline{AB}$ be the base of the triangle. Place
endpoint C on top of endpoint B and
endpoint E on top of endpoint A. These will
become two of the vertices of the triangle.

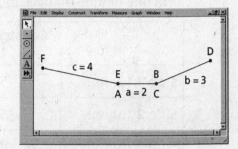

Step 3: Using the endpoints C and E as fixed
vertices, rotate endpoints F and D to see
if they will meet in a single point.

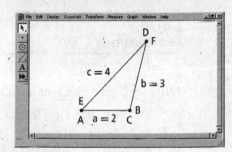

The line segments of 2, 3, and 4 units do /do not
form a triangle.

3a. Repeat Steps 2 and 3, but start with a different base length. Do the line segments make
the exact same triangle as the original?

_____

_____

3b. Use geometry software to draw a triangle with given sides of 2, 3, and 6 units. Do these
line segments form a triangle?

_____

_____

3c. Conjecture When you are given three side lengths that form a triangle,
do you get a unique triangle or more than one triangle?

_____

_____

1. On a separate piece of paper, draw a triangle that has side lengths of 3 cm and 6 cm with an included angle of 120°. Determine if the given information makes a unique triangle, more than one triangle, or no triangle.

_____

_____

2. Use geometry software to determine if the given side lengths can be used to form one unique triangle, more than one triangle, or no triangle.

	Construction 1	Construction 2	Construction 3	Construction 4
Side 1 (units)	5	8	20	1
Side 2 (units)	5	9	20	1
Side 3 (units)	10	10	20	7
Triangle Formation?				

3. On a separate piece of paper, draw a triangle that has degrees of 30°, 60°, and 90°. Measure the side lengths.

   a. Can you draw another triangle with the same angles but different side lengths?

   _____

   _____

   b. If you are given 3 angles in one triangle, will the triangle be unique?

   _____

   _____

4. Draw a freehand sketch of a triangle with three angles that have the same measure. Explain how you made your drawing.

   _____

   _____

   _____

   _____

Cross Sections

COMMON
CORE

CC.7.G.3

Essential question: *How can you identify cross sections of three-dimensional figures?*

An **intersection** is a point or set of points common to two or more geometric figures. A **cross section** is the intersection of a three-dimensional figure and a plane. Below are two examples of cross sections.

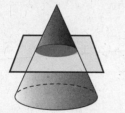

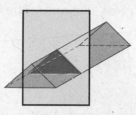

This is figure shows the intersection of the cone and a plane. The cross section is a circle.

This is figure shows the intersection of a triangular prism and a plane. The cross section is a triangle.

A three-dimensional figure can have several different cross-sections depending on the position and the direction of the slice. For example, if the intersection of the plane and cone were vertical, the cross section would from a triangle.

---

1 EXPLORE Cross Sections of a Right Rectangular Prism

Describe each cross section of the right rectangular prism with the name of its shape.

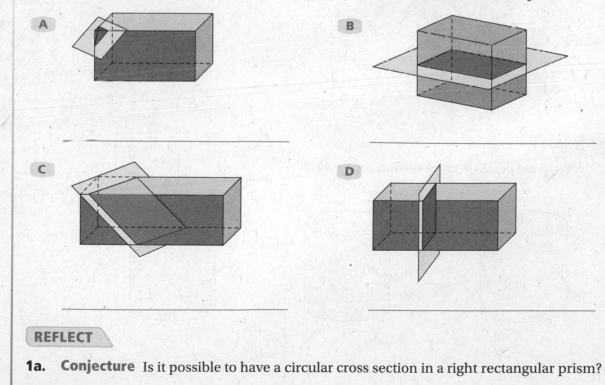

A _____

B _____

C _____

D _____

REFLECT

1a. Conjecture Is it possible to have a circular cross section in a right rectangular prism?

_____

A right rectangular pyramid is shown.

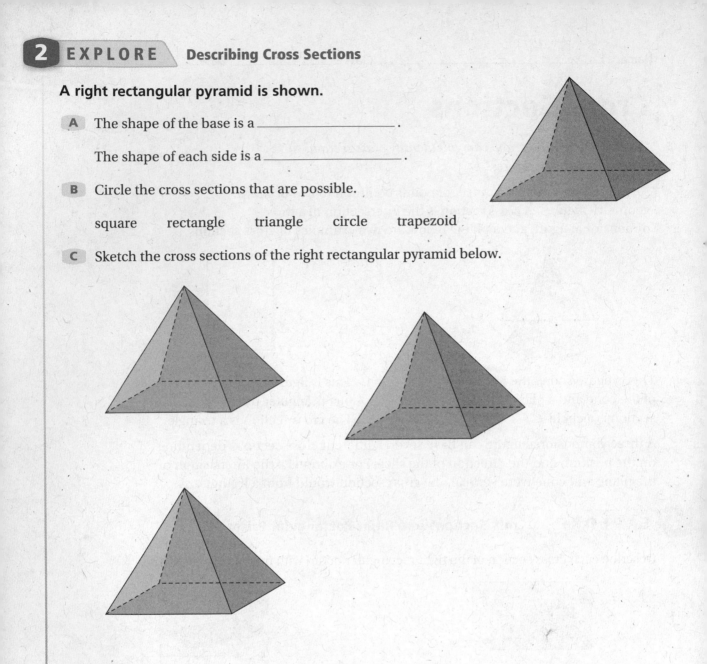

A The shape of the base is a _____ .

The shape of each side is a _____ .

B Circle the cross sections that are possible.

square   rectangle   triangle   circle   trapezoid

C Sketch the cross sections of the right rectangular pyramid below.

TRY THIS!

2a. Draw three possible cross sections of a cylinder.

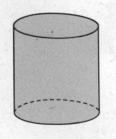
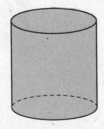
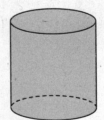

Angle Pairs

COMMON
CORE

CC.7.G.5

Essential question: *How can you use angle pairs to solve problems?*

Recall that two rays with a common endpoint form an angle. The
two rays form the sides of the angle, and the common endpoint
marks the vertex. You can name an angle several ways: by its
vertex, by a point on each ray and the vertex, or by a number.

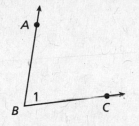

Angle names: ∠ABC, ∠CBA, ∠B, ∠1

It is useful to work with pairs of angles and to understand how
pairs of angles relate to each other. **Congruent angles** are angles
that have the same measure.

1 EXPLORE   Measuring Angles

A   Using a ruler, draw a pair of intersecting lines. Label each angle from 1 to 4.

B   Use a protractor to help you complete the chart.

Angle	Measure of Angle
m∠1	
m∠2	
m∠3	
m∠4	
m∠1 + m∠2	
m∠2 + m∠3	
m∠3 + m∠4	
m∠4 + m∠1	

REFLECT

1a. **Conjecture** Share your results with other students. Make a conjecture about
pairs of angles that are opposite of each other. Make a conjecture about pairs
of angles that are next to each other.

_____

_____

Vertical angles are the opposite angles formed by two intersecting lines. Vertical angles are congruent because the angles have the same measure. **Adjacent angles** are pairs of angles that share a vertex and one side but do not overlap.

Complementary angles are two angles whose measures have a sum of 90°. **Supplementary angles** are two angles whose measures have a sum of 180°. You have discovered in Explore 1 that adjacent angles formed by two intersecting lines are supplementary.

2 EXAMPLE   Identifying Angles and Angle Pairs

Use the diagram below.

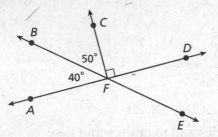

A   Name a pair of adjacent angles. _____

B   Name a pair of vertical angles. _____

C   Name a pair of complementary angles. _____

D   Name an angle that is supplementary to ∠CFE: _____

E   Name an angle that is supplementary to ∠BFD. _____

F   Name an angle that is supplementary to ∠CFD. _____

G   Name a pair of non-adjacent angles that are complementary. _____

REFLECT

2a.   What is the measure of ∠DFE? Explain how you found the measure.

_____

_____

2b.   Are ∠CFB and ∠DFE vertical angles? Why or why not?

_____

_____

2c.   Are ∠BFD and ∠AFE vertical angles? Why or why not?

_____

_____

Find the measure of each angle.

A   ∠BDC

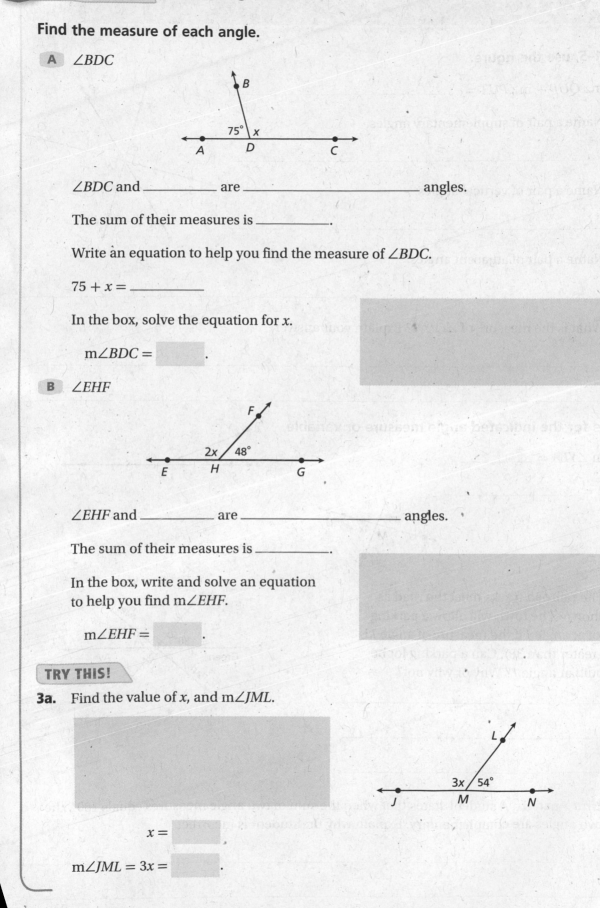

∠BDC and _____ are _____ angles.

The sum of their measures is _____.

Write an equation to help you find the measure of ∠BDC.

75 + x = _____

In the box, solve the equation for x.

m∠BDC = [ ] .

B   ∠EHF

∠EHF and _____ are _____ angles.

The sum of their measures is _____.

In the box, write and solve an equation
to help you find m∠EHF.

m∠EHF = [ ] .

TRY THIS!

3a.   Find the value of x, and m∠JML.

x = [ ]

m∠JML = 3x = [ ] .

PRACTICE

For 1–5, use the figure.

1. m∠QUP + m∠PUT = _____

2. Name a pair of supplementary angles.

   _____

3. Name a pair of vertical angles.

   _____

4. Name a pair of adjacent angles.

   _____

5. What is the measure of ∠QUN? Explain your answer.

   _____

   _____

Solve for the indicated angle measure or variable.

6. m ∠YLA = _____

7. $x =$ _____

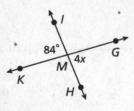

8. The railroad tracks meet the road as shown. The town will allow a parking lot at angle J if the measure of angle J is greater than 38°. Can a parking lot be built at angle J? Why or why not?

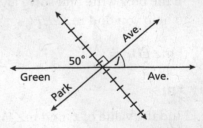

   _____

   _____

   _____

9. **Error Analysis** A student states that when the sum of two angle measures equals 180°, the two angles are complementary. Explain why the student is incorrect.

   _____

   _____

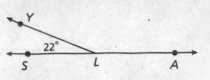

Problem Solving Connections 🌐

Buying a Home Tina and Raul are buying a new house. The blueprint shows the layout of the bottom floor of the home and its backyard.

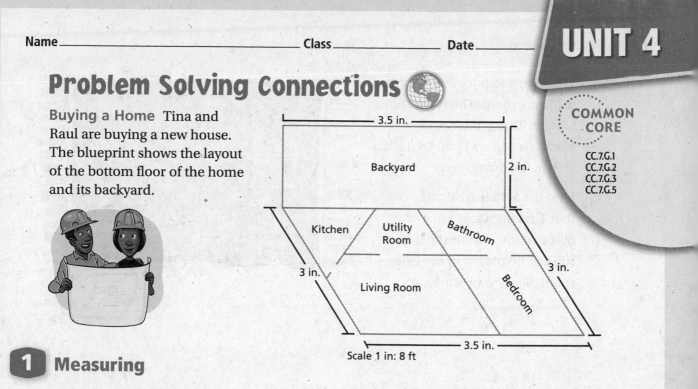

Scale 1 in: 8 ft

1 Measuring

A Complete the table.

Blueprint length (in.)	1	1.5	2	2.5	3	3.5	4
Actual length (ft)	8	12					

B Use the table to find the find the given lengths.

Front of house: _____ ft   Length of backyard: _____ ft

Sides of house: _____ ft   Width of backyard: _____ ft

C Tina and Raul want to put a fence around the backyard. How much fencing do they need?

_____

D Also in the backyard Raul decides to put down a path from the back door straight across the yard to the fence. Each square stone has a length of 0.5 feet. How many stones will fit across the yard? Show your work below.

E Tina wants to place a shelving unit in the utility room along the back wall. The unit she has is 7 feet in length. Will the shelving unit fit along the back wall of the utility room if it measures 0.75 inches in the blueprint? Explain.

_____

2 Decorating

A Tina wants to put a large rug in the living room. The rug is shown at right. Tina estimates she can place a rug in an $1\frac{1}{2}$ in.-by-$1\frac{1}{2}$ in. area in the living room.

Find the actual area of the rug that Tina thinks will fit in the living room. Determine if her rug can be placed in the living room. Show your work.

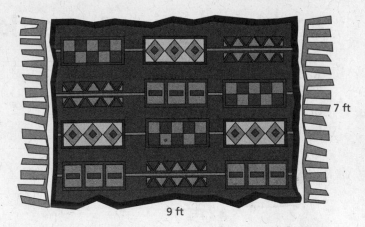

7 ft

9 ft

B Tina and Raul need to put down grass in the backyard. Find the area of the backyard. Show your work.

C If grass comes in rectangles that have an area of 8 square feet, how many rectangles do they need to buy? Find the total cost of the grass if each rectangle costs $1.25 and sales tax is 8%. Show your work below.

3 Building

A Raul is going to build a small triangular table to place in the corner of the bedroom as shown on the blueprint. The angle of the corner is 60°. Raul wants the side against the bathroom wall to be $1\frac{1}{2}$ feet long and the front side facing the bedroom to be 2 feet long. Is this triangular table possible to build? Show your work.

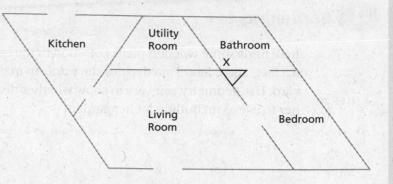

B In what other corner of the house could this table be placed? Mark it on the blue print and explain why it could fit there.

_____

_____

C Tina decides she wants the side of the table that faces the bedroom to be 1 foot in length. Is it possible for Raul to build this table? Show your work and explain your answer.

D If Raul wants to build a shelf to fit into the corner of the bathroom marked with an "x" on the blueprint, what would be the measure of the angle in the corner? Explain.

_____

_____

4 Gardening

A   Raul finds some wooden planks of wood in the backyard with lengths 6 feet, 6.5 feet, and 8 feet. Tina decides she wants to make a triangular garden in the yard. Use geometry software to show whether these planks form a triangle for her to use as an outline for her garden.

B   If Tina can form a triangle, will it only be one shape and size or can she make a different shape and size out of the planks?

_____

_____

C   Raul also finds a block of wood in the shape of a cube with a 6-foot side length. He is going to use the wood to cut the top of a patio table. Could he cut a cross section of the block to form an equilateral triangle? What about a triangle that is not equilateral? Show your work below.

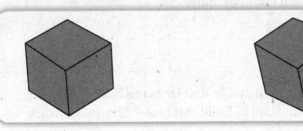

D   If Raul cuts through all six faces of the cube, what is the resulting shape of the cross section?

_____

E   Name and draw 3 other possible cross sections that Raul could cut for his patio table top. Could Raul cut a circular cross section?

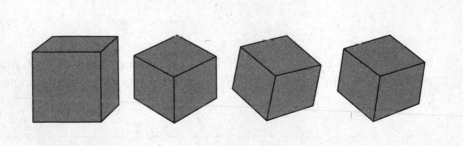

Name _____ Class _____ Date _____

MULTIPLE CHOICE

1. Which of the following could be a horizontal cross-section of a cylinder?

  A. hexagon   **C.** circle

  B. triangle   **D.** octagon

2. If two angles are supplementary, what is the sum of their measures?

  F. 30°   **H.** 180°

  G. 90°   **J.** 360°

3. What is the measure of the angle that is complementary to the angle shown?

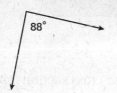

  A. 2°   **C.** 90°

  B. 12°   **D.** 92°

4. A map has a scale of 1 inch to 5 miles. The distance from Yuri's home to school is 10 miles. How many inches is Yuri's home from school on the map?

  F. 1 inch   **H.** 5 inches

  G. 2 inches   **J.** 10 inches

5. Angle D is a vertical angle to ∠F. The measure of ∠D is 53°. What is the measure of ∠F?

  A. 3°   **C.** 43°

  B. 37°   **D.** 53°

6. Which of the following could NOT be a cross section of a rectangular prism?

  F. rectangle   **H.** parallelogram

  G. circle   **J.** triangle

Use the figure for problems 7–11.

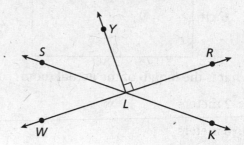

7. Which pair of angles are adjacent angles?

  A. ∠SLW and ∠RLK

  B. ∠SLW and ∠WLK

  C. ∠SLY and ∠WLK

  D. ∠YLR and ∠YLK

8. Which pair of adjacent angles are supplementary angles?

  F. ∠RLK and ∠YLR

  G. ∠SLY and ∠YLR

  H. ∠RLK and ∠WLK

  J. ∠SLW and ∠WLR

9. Which pair of angles are complementary angles?

  A. ∠YLS and ∠RLK

  B. ∠YLR and ∠YLS

  C. ∠SLW and ∠RLK

  D. ∠WLK and ∠RLK

10. The measure of ∠RLK is 38°. What is the measure of ∠SLY?

  F. 52°   **H.** 142°

  G. 62°   **J.** 218°

11. The sum of which two angle measures equals the measure of ∠WLK?

  A. ∠SLY and ∠YLR

  B. ∠SLW and ∠YLR

  C. ∠RLK and ∠SLY

  D. ∠RLK and ∠YLR

The figure is a scale drawing of a rectangular room. The scale is 2 cm:4 m. Use the figure for problems 12–14.

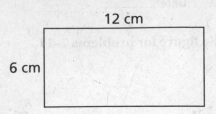

12 cm

6 cm

12. What is the length of the actual room?

  F. 2 meters

  G. 6 meters

  H. 12 meters

  J. 24 meters

13. What is the width of the actual room?

  A. 6 meters

  B. 12 meters

  C. 18 meters

  D. 24 meters

14. What is the area of the actual room?

  F. 72 square meters

  G. 144 square meters

  H. 288 square meters

  J. 576 square meters

FREE RESPONSE

Use the figure for problems 15 and 16.

15. Write and solve an equation to find the measure of $\angle TSU$.

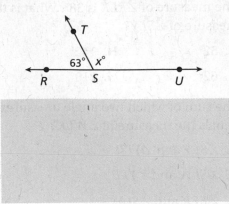

T

63° $x°$

R S U

16. Name two ways to describe angles TSU and TSR. Explain.

_____

_____

_____

_____

_____

_____

17. What shape describes the cross section in the cube below?

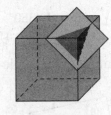

_____

18. Name 2 other cross sections shapes that can be made from the cube.

_____

_____

_____

19. Draw a triangle with angle measures of 32°, and 45°, and an included side with a length of 2 inches.

Geometry: Circumference, Area, and Volume

Unit Focus

While you have worked with and found areas of triangles and quadrilaterals, now you will find the area of circles and composite figures. You will also discover a relationship between the ratio of the circumference to the diameter of a circle. This relationship is represented by the Greek letter, π. Then, you will apply your understanding of area to solve area and surface area problems. In addition, you will find the volume of different prisms.

Unit at a Glance

COMMON CORE

UNIT 5

Unpacking the Common Core State Standards

Use the table to help you understand the Standards for Mathematical Content that are taught in this unit. Refer to the lessons listed after each standard for exploration and practice.

COMMON CORE Standards for Mathematical Content	What It Means For You
CC.7.G.4 Know the formulas for the area and circumference of a circle and use them to solve problems; give an informal derivation of the relationship between the circumference and area of a circle. Lessons 5-1, 5-2	Given any circle, you will be able to find its circumference and area. You will understand the difference between area and circumference and their formulas. You will also learn the relationship between the circumference and area of a circle. Then, you will solve problems by applying your knowledge of circles.
CC.7.G.6 Solve real-world and mathematical problems involving area, volume, and surface area of two- and three-dimensional objects composed of triangles, quadrilaterals, polygons, cubes, and right prisms. Lessons 5-3, 5-4, 5-5	You will solve problems by using formulas to find the areas, surface areas, and volumes of two- and three-dimensional figures. They may be simple or composite figures made up of triangles, quadrilaterals, polygons, cubes, and right prisms.

Circumference of a Circle

Essential question: *How do you find the circumference of a circle?*

COMMON CORE

CC.7.G.4

Remember that a circle is a set of points in a plane that are a fixed distance from the center.

The **diameter** of a circle is a line segment that passes through the center of the circle and whose endpoints lie on the circle.

The **radius** is a line segment with one endpoint at the center of the circle and the other endpoint on the circle.

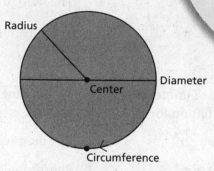

The **circumference** of a circle is the distance around the circle.

1 EXPLORE   Exploring Circumference

A Use a measuring tape to find the circumference of five circular objects. Then measure the distance across each item to find its diameter. Record the measurements of each object in the table below.

Object	Circumference C	Diameter d	$\frac{C}{d}$

B Divide the circumference of each object by its diameter. Round your answer to the nearest hundredth.

C Describe what you notice about the ratio $\frac{C}{d}$ in your table.

_____

REFLECT

1a. **Conjecture** Compare your results with other students. Make a conjecture about the relationship between the circumference and the diameter of a circle.

_____

1b. How could you estimate the circumference of a circular object without measuring it if you know the diameter?

_____

The ratio of the circumference to the diameter $\frac{C}{d}$ of any circle is the same for all circles. The ratio is called *pi*, or π. As you calculated in ❶, the value of π is close to 3. You can approximate π as 3.14 or $\frac{22}{7}$. You can use this ratio to find a formula for circumference.

For any circle, $\frac{C}{d} = \pi$. Solve the equation for C to give an equation for the circumference of a circle in terms of the diameter.

$\frac{C}{d} = \pi$ The ratio of _____ to _____ is *pi*.

$\frac{C}{d} \times \boxed{} = \pi \times \boxed{}$ Multiply both sides by _____.

$C = $ _____   Simplify.

Since the diameter is the same as two times the radius, you can also substitute $2r$ in the equation for d.

$d = 2r$ The diameter is two times the _____.

$C = \pi\left(\boxed{} \right)$ Substitute for d.

$C = 2\pi r$ Use the Commutative Property.

The two equivalent formulas for circumference are:

$C = \boxed{}$ and $C = \boxed{}$

2 EXAMPLE   **Finding the Circumference of a Circle**

Find the circumference of the circle to the nearest hundredth. Use 3.14 for π.

The _____ of the circle is 3 cm. Use the formula that includes the radius, _____.

$C = 2\pi \boxed{}$ *Use the formula.*

$C = 2\pi \boxed{}$ *Substitute 3 for r.*

$C \approx 2\left(\boxed{} \right)(3)$ *Substitute 3.14 for π.*

$C \approx \boxed{}$ *Multiply.*

The circumference is about _____ cm.

REFLECT

2a. What value of *pi* could you use to estimate the circumference? _____

2b. How do you know your answer is reasonable?

_____

2c. When would it be logical to use $\frac{22}{7}$ instead of 3.14 for *pi*?

_____

The circumference of a circular pond is 942 feet. A model boat is moving directly across the pond, along the diameter, at a rate of 4 feet per second. How long does it take the boat to get to the other side?

A Make a diagram.

Sketch the pond, and label what you know and what you need to find.

B First, you need to find the diameter of the pond. Use the formula for circumference, and solve for d.

$C = \boxed{}$ *Write the formula.*

$\boxed{} \approx \boxed{}\, d$ *Substitute for the circumference and pi.*

$\dfrac{942}{\boxed{}} \approx \dfrac{3.14d}{}$ *Divide both sides by* _____.

$\boxed{} \approx d$ *Simplify.*

The diameter is about _____ feet.

C Find the time it takes the boat to get across the pond traveling along the diameter.

Divide the length of the diameter by the boat's speed.

$\boxed{} \div \boxed{} = \boxed{}$

It takes the boat _____ seconds to get across.

REFLECT

3a. What If? How long would it take the boat to get across the pond if the model boat traveled at a rate of 5 feet per second?

_____

TRY THIS!

3b. The circumference of a circular garden is 42 meters. A gardener is using a machine to dig a straight line along the diameter of the garden at a rate of 10 meters per hour. How many hours will it take the gardener to dig across the garden?

_____

PRACTICE

Find the circumference of each circle to the nearest tenth, if necessary. Use 3.14 or $\frac{22}{7}$ for π.

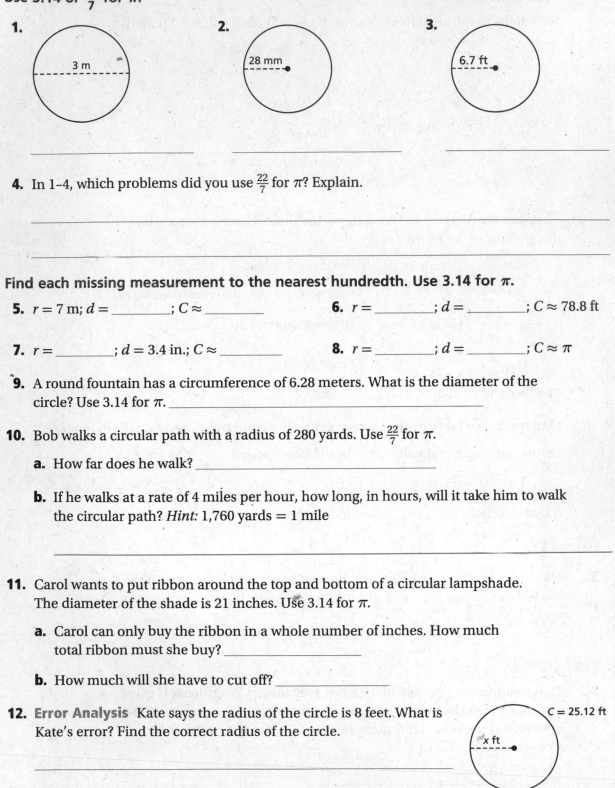

1.

3 m

_____

2.

28 mm

_____

3.

6.7 ft

_____

4. In 1–4, which problems did you use $\frac{22}{7}$ for π? Explain.

_____

_____

Find each missing measurement to the nearest hundredth. Use 3.14 for π.

5. $r = 7$ m; $d =$ _____; $C \approx$ _____

6. $r =$ _____; $d =$ _____; $C \approx 78.8$ ft

7. $r =$ _____; $d = 3.4$ in.; $C \approx$ _____

8. $r =$ _____; $d =$ _____; $C \approx \pi$

9. A round fountain has a circumference of 6.28 meters. What is the diameter of the circle? Use 3.14 for π. _____

10. Bob walks a circular path with a radius of 280 yards. Use $\frac{22}{7}$ for π.

  a. How far does he walk? _____

  b. If he walks at a rate of 4 miles per hour, how long, in hours, will it take him to walk the circular path? *Hint:* 1,760 yards = 1 mile

_____

11. Carol wants to put ribbon around the top and bottom of a circular lampshade. The diameter of the shade is 21 inches. Use 3.14 for π.

  a. Carol can only buy the ribbon in a whole number of inches. How much total ribbon must she buy? _____

  b. How much will she have to cut off? _____

12. Error Analysis Kate says the radius of the circle is 8 feet. What is Kate's error? Find the correct radius of the circle.

$C = 25.12$ ft

x ft

_____

_____

Name _____ Class _____ Date _____

Area of a Circle

Essential question: *How do you find the area of a circle?*

COMMON CORE

CC.7.G.4

1 E X P L O R E   Finding the Area of a Circle

You can use what you know about circles and *pi* to help find the formula for the area of a circle.

Step 1: Use a compass to draw a circle and cut it out.

Step 2: Fold the circle three times as shown to get equal wedges.

Step 3: Unfold and shade one-half of the circle.

Step 4: Cut out the wedges and fit the pieces together to form a figure that looks like a parallelogram.

The base and height of the parallelogram relate to the parts of the circle.

Radius

Half the circumference

base $b =$ ____ the circumference of the circle, or _____

height $h =$ the _____ of the circle, or _____

To find the area of a parallelogram, the equation is $A =$ _____.

To find the area of the circle, substitute for b and h in the area formula.

$A = bh$

$A = \boxed{}\, h$ *Substitute πr for b.*

$A = \pi r \boxed{}$ *Substitute r for h.*

$A = \pi \boxed{}$ *$r \cdot r = r^2$*

REFLECT

1a. Conjecture Make a conjecture about the lengths of all the radii of a circle.

_____

1b. How can you make the wedges look more like a parallelogram?

_____

_____

Area of a Circle

The area of a circle is equal to π times the radius squared.

$$A = \pi r^2$$

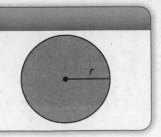

Remember that area is given in square units.

2 EXAMPLE   Finding the Area of a Circle

A biscuit recipe calls for the dough to be rolled out and circles to be cut from the dough. The biscuit cutter used is shown. Find the area of the biscuit once it is cut. Use 3.14 for π.

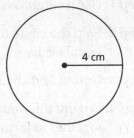

4 cm

$A = \pi \boxed{}^{\boxed{}}$	*Use the formula.*
$A = \pi \boxed{}^2$	*Substitute. Use 4 for r.*
$A \approx \boxed{} \times 4^2$	*Substitute. Use 3.14 for π.*
$A \approx 3.14 \times \boxed{}$	*Evaluate the power.*
$A \approx \boxed{}$	*Multiply.*

The area of the biscuit is about _____.

TRY THIS!

2a. A flower garden is in the shape of a circle with a diameter of 10 yards. What is the area of the garden? Use 3.14 for π.

The area of the garden is about _____.

2b. A circular pool has a radius of 10 feet. What is the area of the pool? Use 3.14 for π.

The area of the pool is about _____.

REFLECT

2c. Compare finding the area of a circle when given the radius with finding the area when given the diameter.

_____

_____

2d. How you could estimate or check the reasonableness of an answer for the area of a circle?

_____

2e. Why do you evaluate the power in the equation before multiplying?

_____

_____

You can use what you know about circumference and area of circles to find a relationship between them.

Find the relationship between the circumference and area of a circle.

Start with a circle that has radius r.

Solve the equation $C = 2\pi r$ for r.

$$r = \frac{\boxed{}}{\boxed{}}$$

Substitute your expression for r in the formula for area of a circle.

$$A = \pi \left(\frac{\boxed{}}{\boxed{}} \right)^2$$

Square the term in the parenthesis.

$$A = \pi \left(\frac{\boxed{}^2}{\boxed{}^2 \cdot \boxed{}^2} \right)$$

Evaluate the power.

$$A = \frac{\boxed{} \cdot \boxed{}^2}{\boxed{} \cdot \boxed{}^2}$$

Simplify.

$$A = \frac{\boxed{}^2}{\boxed{} \cdot \boxed{}}$$

Solve for C^2.

$$C^2 = 4\boxed{}\boxed{}$$

The circumference of the circle squared is equal to _____.

REFLECT

3a. Does this formula work for a circle with a radius of 3 inches? Show your work below.

TRY THIS!

Find the area of the circles given the circumference. Give your answers in terms of π.

3b. $C = 8\pi;\ A = $ _____

3c. $C = \pi;\ A = $ _____

3d. $C = 2\pi;\ A = $ _____

Find the area of each circle to the nearest tenth, if necessary. Use 3.14 for π.

1.

14 m

_____

2.

12 mm

_____

3.

20 yd

_____

4.

5 ft

_____

5.

6.4 cm

_____

6.

8.25 in.

_____

7. A clock face has a radius of 8 inches. What is the area of the clock face? Round your answer to the nearest hundredth.

_____

8. A DVD has a diameter of 12 centimeters. What is the area of the DVD? Round your answer to the nearest hundredth.

_____

9. A company makes steel lids that have a diameter of 13 inches. What is the area of each lid? Round your answer to the nearest hundredth.

_____

10. A circular garden has an area of 64π square yards. What is the circumference of the garden? Give your answer in terms of π.

_____

11. **Reasoning** A small silver dollar pancake served at a restuarant has a circumference of 2π inches. A regular pancake has a circumference of 4π inches. Is the area of the regular pancake twice the area of the silver dollar pancake? Explain.

_____

_____

12. **Critical Thinking** Describe another way to find the area of a circle when given the circumference.

_____

_____

5-3

Solving Area Problems

Essential question: *How do you find the area of composite figures?*

COMMON
CORE

CC.7.G.6

1 EXPLORE   Area of a Composite Figure

Aaron was plotting the shape of his garden on grid
paper. While it was an irregular shape, it was perfect
for his yard. Each square on the grid represents
1 square meter.

A   Describe one way you can find the area
of this garden.

_____

_____

_____

B   The area of the garden is _____ square meters.

C   Compare your results with other students. What other methods were used to find the area?

_____

_____

_____

D   How does your area compare with the area found using different methods?

_____

REFLECT

1.   Use dotted lines to show two different ways Aaron's garden could be divided up into simple
geometric figures.

A composite figure is made up of simple geometric shapes. To find the area of composite figures and other irregular shaped figures, divide it into simple, non-overlapping figures. Find the area of each simpler figure, and then add them together to find the total area of the composite figure.

Use the chart below to review some common area formulas.

Shape	Area Formula
triangle	$A = \frac{1}{2}bh$
square	$A = s^2$
rectangle	$A = \ell w$
parallelogram	$A = bh$
trapezoid	$A = \frac{1}{2}h(b_1 + b_2)$

2 **EXAMPLE**   **Finding the Area of a Composite Figure**

Find the area of the figure.

A Into what two figures can you divide this composite figure?

_____

B Find the area of each shape.

Area of the Parallelogram

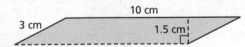

The base of the parallelogram is _____ cm.

The height of the parallelogram is _____ cm.

Use the formula.

$A = bh$

$A = $ ▢ $\cdot$ ▢

$A = $ ▢

The area of the parallelogram is _____ cm².

Area of the Trapezoid

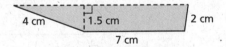

The bottom base of the trapezoid is _____ cm.

The top base the trapezoid is _____ cm, since it is the same length as the base of the parallelogram.

The height of the trapezoid is _____ cm.

Use the formula.

$A = \frac{1}{2}h(b_1 + b_2)$

$A = \frac{1}{2}$ ▢ $\left(▢ + ▢\right)$

$A = \frac{1}{2}$ ▢ $\left(▢\right)$

$A = $ ▢

The area of the trapezoid is _____ cm².

C Find the area of the composite figure.

_____ + _____ = _____
   Area of parallelogram   Area of trapezoid   Area of composite shape

REFLECT

2a. Describe another way to divide the shape into simpler figures.

_____

2b. If you divide the composite figure into different shapes, what is the area? What does this tell you?

_____

_____

3 **EXAMPLE**   Calculating Cost Based on Area

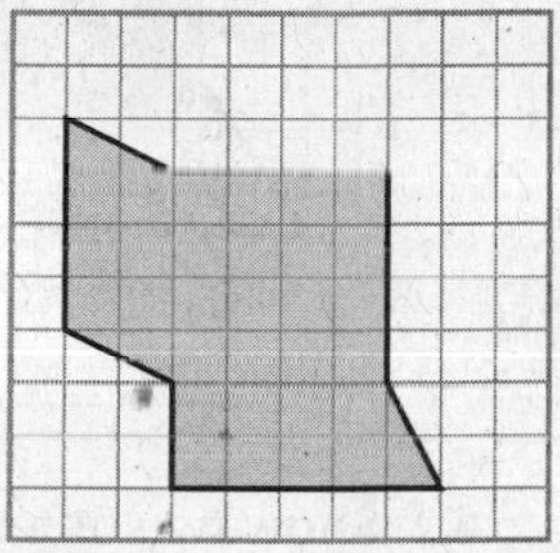

A banquet room is being carpeted. A floor plan of the room is shown at right. Each unit length represents 1 yard. Carpet costs $23.50 per square yard. How much will it cost to carpet the room?

A Divide the figure into simpler shapes: a parallelogram, a rectangle, and a triangle. Show the divisions on the floor plan with dotted lines. Count the units to find the dimensions.

B Find the area of the parallelogram.

$A = bh$

$A = $ ▭ $\cdot$ ▭

$A = $ ▭ square yards

C Find the area of the rectangle.

$A = \ell w$

$A = $ ▭ $\cdot$ ▭

$A = $ ▭ square yards

D Find the area of the triangle.

$A = \frac{1}{2}bh$

$A = \frac{1}{2}$ ▭ $\cdot$ ▭

$A = $ ▭ square yard

E The area of the composite figure is _____ yd^2.

F To calculate the cost to carpet the room, multiply _____ by the _____.

The cost to carpet the banquet room is _____.

3. Describe how you can estimate the cost to carpet the room.

_____

_____

_____

PRACTICE

Find the area of each figure. Use 3.14 for π.

1.

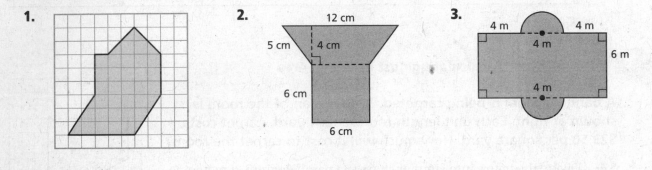

2.

12 cm

5 cm | 4 cm

6 cm

6 cm

3.

4 m   4 m
4 m
6 m
4 m

_____

_____

_____

4. Show two different ways to divide the composite figure.
Find the area both ways. Show your work below.

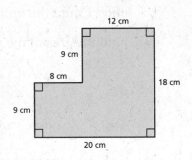

12 cm
9 cm
8 cm
18 cm
9 cm
20 cm

5. Sal is tiling his entryway. The floor plan is drawn
on a unit grid. Each unit length represents 1 foot.
Tile costs $2.25 per square foot. How much will Sal
pay to tile his entryway?

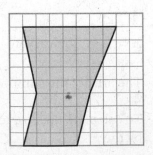

_____

6. **Reasoning** A composite figure is formed by
combining a square and a triangle. Its total area
is 32.5 ft². The area of the triangle is 7.5 ft². What
is the length of each side of the square?

_____

Solving Surface Area Problems

Essential question: *How do you find the surface area of a figure made of prisms?*

1 EXPLORE Comparing the Surface Area of Two Figures

Using centimeter cubes, build the two figures shown.

A Find the surface area of the 3-by-3-by-3 cube.

_____

B Now find the surface area of the cube with one missing corner.

_____

C Which figure has a greater surface area: the 3-by-3-by-3 cube, or the same cube with one of the corners missing?

_____

REFLECT

1a. How did you find the surface area of the figures?

_____

_____

1b. Why does it make sense that the surface areas are equal?

_____

_____

1c. **What If?** If four cubes are taken, one from each corner of the top layer, would this change the surface area?

_____

_____

One way to find the surface area of a figure is to make a net, open it up, find the areas of the shapes, and add them together. Another way to find the surface area is to use a formula.

Consider a rectangular prism with length, ℓ, width, w, and height, h. The top and bottom faces have the same area, $A = \boxed{}$. The front and back faces have the same area, $A = \boxed{}h$. The left and right faces have the same area, $A = w\boxed{}$.

To find the surface area, add the areas of the top, bottom, front, back, left, and right faces.

$$S = \boxed{} + \boxed{} + \boxed{} + \boxed{} + \boxed{} + \boxed{}$$

$$\text{top} \quad \text{bottom} \quad \text{front} \quad \text{back} \quad \text{left} \quad \text{right}$$

Combine like terms to find the formula for surface area of a rectangular prism.

$$S = 2\boxed{} + 2\boxed{} + 2\boxed{}$$

2 EXAMPLE Finding the Surface Area of a Rectangular Prism

Felix is making a jewelry box out of balsa wood as a present for his sister. He wants the jewelry box to be 12 inches long, 4 inches wide, and 6 inches tall. How much balsa wood does Felix need?

Step 1: Sketch and label the prism.

Step 2: Find how much balsa wood Felix needs to make his box.

- Use the formula for surface area of a rectangular prism.
  $S = 2\ell w + 2\ell h + 2wh$

- Substitute for the length, width, and height.
  $$S = 2\left(\boxed{} \cdot \boxed{} \right) + 2\left(\boxed{} \cdot \boxed{} \right) + 2\left(\boxed{} \cdot \boxed{} \right)$$

- Simplify each term.
  $$S = \boxed{} + \boxed{} + \boxed{}$$

- Add.
  $$S = \boxed{}$$

Felix needs _____ of balsa wood for his jewelry box.

REFLECT

2. Adapt the formula for the surface area of a rectangular prism for a cube. What is the formula for the surface area of a cube?

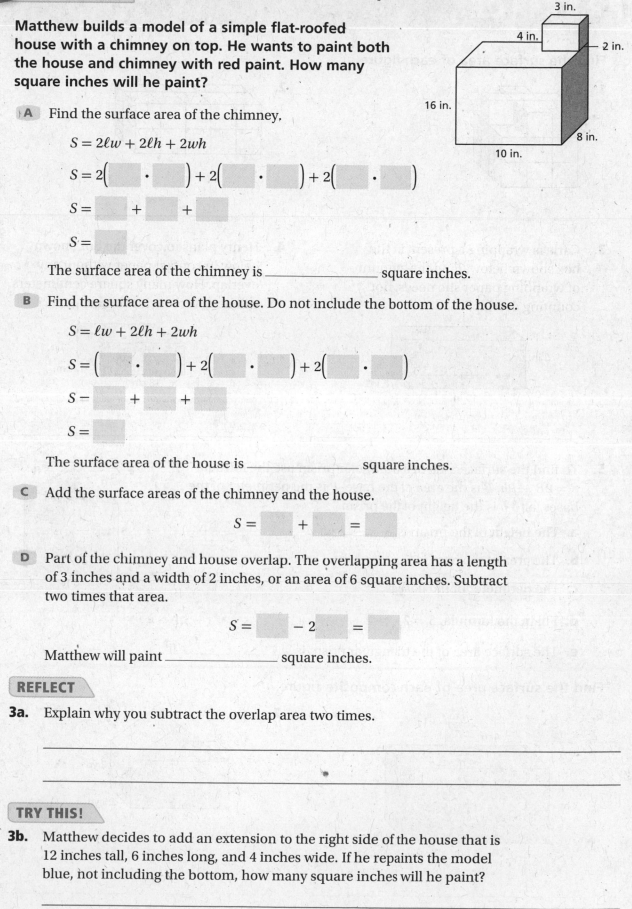

3 EXAMPLE   Finding the Surface Area of a Composite Solid

Matthew builds a model of a simple flat-roofed house with a chimney on top. He wants to paint both the house and chimney with red paint. How many square inches will he paint?

A   Find the surface area of the chimney.

$$S = 2\ell w + 2\ell h + 2wh$$

$$S = 2\left(\boxed{} \cdot \boxed{}\right) + 2\left(\boxed{} \cdot \boxed{}\right) + 2\left(\boxed{} \cdot \boxed{}\right)$$

$$S = \boxed{} + \boxed{} + \boxed{}$$

$$S = \boxed{}$$

The surface area of the chimney is _____ square inches.

B   Find the surface area of the house. Do not include the bottom of the house.

$$S = \ell w + 2\ell h + 2wh$$

$$S = \left(\boxed{} \cdot \boxed{}\right) + 2\left(\boxed{} \cdot \boxed{}\right) + 2\left(\boxed{} \cdot \boxed{}\right)$$

$$S = \boxed{} + \boxed{} + \boxed{}$$

$$S = \boxed{}$$

The surface area of the house is _____ square inches.

C   Add the surface areas of the chimney and the house.

$$S = \boxed{} + \boxed{} = \boxed{}$$

D   Part of the chimney and house overlap. The overlapping area has a length of 3 inches and a width of 2 inches, or an area of 6 square inches. Subtract two times that area.

$$S = \boxed{} - 2\boxed{} = \boxed{}$$

Matthew will paint _____ square inches.

REFLECT

3a. Explain why you subtract the overlap area two times.

_____

_____

TRY THIS!

3b. Matthew decides to add an extension to the right side of the house that is 12 inches tall, 6 inches long, and 4 inches wide. If he repaints the model blue, not including the bottom, how many square inches will he paint?

_____

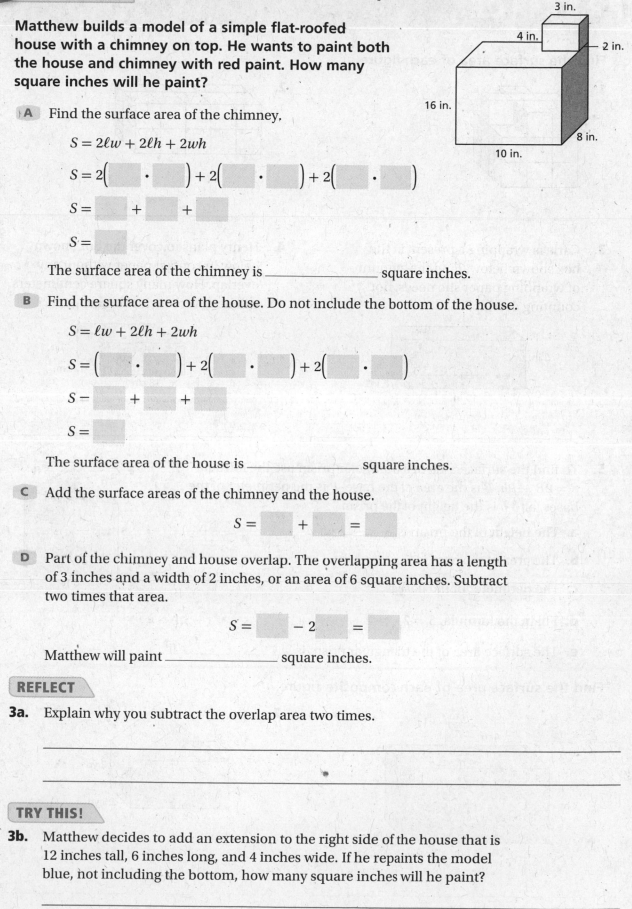

Find the surface area of each figure.

1.

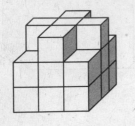

2.

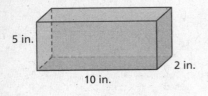

3. Carla is wrapping a present in the box shown below. Find the amount of wrapping paper she needs, not counting overlap.

4. Henry plans to cover the box shown below in contact paper without any overlap. How many square centimeters will be covered with contact paper?

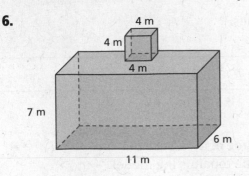

5 in.

2 in.

10 in.

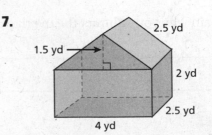

10 cm

12 cm

18 cm

5. To find the surface area of a triangular prism use the formula $S = 2B + Ph$. B is the area of the base, P is the perimeter of the bases, and h is the height of the prism.

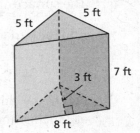

5 ft

5 ft

7 ft

3 ft

8 ft

a. The height of the prism is _____ ft.

b. The area of the base is _____ ft².

c. The perimeter of the base is _____ ft.

d. Fill in the formula. $S = 2 \cdot$ ▢ $+$ ▢

e. The surface area of the triangular prism is _____ ft².

Find the surface area of each composite figure.

6.

4 m

4 m

4 m

7 m

6 m

11 m

7.

2.5 yd

1.5 yd

2 yd

2.5 yd

4 yd

Solving Volume Problems

Essential question: *How do you find the volume of a figure made up of cubes and prisms?*

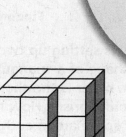

1 EXPLORE   Finding the Volume of a Prism

A Use centimeter cubes to build a prism like the one shown. Each cube represents a unit of measure called a cubic unit, so centimeter cubes represent cubic centimeters.

Step 1: Find the volume of the prism. Count the number of cubes that make up the prism.

The volume of the prism is _____ cm³.

Step 2: Find the area of the base by counting the number of cubes that make up the face of the top or bottom of the prism.

The area of the base is _____ cm².

Step 3: Find the height of the prism.

The height of the prism is _____ cm

Do you see a relationship between the volume and the area of the base and the height of the prism?

_____

B Following the steps in **A**, find the volume, area of the base, and height of the given prism.

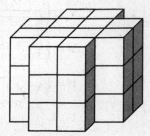

Volume: _____ cm³

Area of the base: _____ cm²

Height of the prism: _____ cm

Do you see a relationship between the volume and the area of the base and the height of the prism?

_____

REFLECT

1a. **Conjecture** Based on your discoveries in **1**, describe in words a way to find the volume of any prism.

_____

You can find the volume of any prism by multiplying the area of the base B by the height of the prism h.

> **Volume of a Prism**
>
> The volume V of a prism is the area of its base B times its height h.
> $$V = Bh$$

2 **EXAMPLE** Finding the Volume of Prisms

Bradley is setting up two tents. One is the shape of a triangular prism and the other is the shape of a trapezoidal prism. How many cubic feet of space are in each tent?

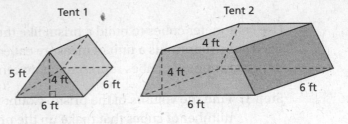

Tent 1   Tent 2

A Find the volume of Tent 1.

$V = \boxed{} h$ *Use the formula.*

$V = \left(\boxed{}\right)h$ *The base is a triangle.*

$V = \left(\dfrac{1}{2}\boxed{}\right)h$ *Substitute for b and h in the base.*

$V = \left(\boxed{}\right)\left(\boxed{}\right)$ *Substitute for the height of the prism, h.*

$V = \boxed{}$ *Multiply.*

The volume of Tent 1 is _____ ft³.

B Find the volume of Tent 2.

$V = \boxed{} h$ *Use the formula.*

$V = \left(\boxed{}\right)h$ *The base is a trapezoid.*

$V = \left(\dfrac{1}{2}\boxed{}\left(\boxed{}\right)\right)h$ *Substitute for h, b_1, and b_2 in the base.*

$V = \left(\boxed{}\right)\left(\boxed{}\right)$ *Substitute for the height of the prism, h.*

$V = \boxed{}$ *Multiply.*

The volume of Tent 2 is _____ ft³.

REFLECT

2. For a prism that is not a rectangular prism, how do you determine which sides are the bases? For a rectangular prism, how do you determine which sides are the bases?

_____

_____

3 EXAMPLE · Finding the Volume of a Composite Solid

Allie has two aquariums connected by a small square prism. Find the
volume of the double aquarium.

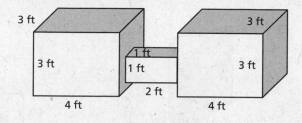

A Find the volume of each of the larger aquariums.

$V = Bh$ *Use the formula.*

$V = \left(\right)\left(\right)$ *Substitute for B and h.*

$V = $ *Multiply.*

The volume of each end aquarium is _____ cubic feet.

B Find the volume of the connecting prism.

$V = Bh$ *Use the formula.*

$V = \left(\right)\left(\right)$ *Substitute for B and h.*

$V = $ *Multiply.*

The volume of the connecting prism is _____ cubic feet.

C Add the volume of each part of the aquarium.

$$V - + + - $$

The volume of the aquarium is _____ cubic feet.

REFLECT

3a. What If? Find the volume of the aquarium if all of the dimensions were doubled.
What is the relationship between the original volume and the new volume?

_____

_____

3b. Find the volume of one of the end aquariums using another pair of opposite
sides as the base. Do you still get the same volume? Explain.

_____

_____

Find the volume of each figure.

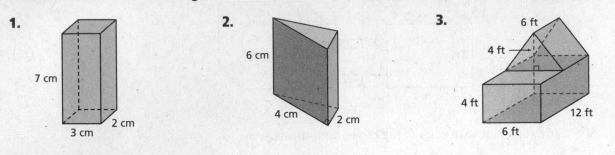

1.

2.

3.

_____   _____   _____

4. Pete fills the container shown with sand. How much sand fills the container?

_____

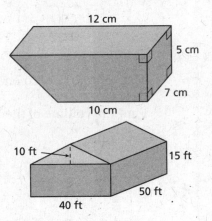

5. Mr. Fowler is building a barn for his farm. The dimensions are shown at right. Find the volume of the entire barn.

_____

6. A movie theater offers popcorn in two different containers for the same price. One container is a rectangular prism with a base area of 36 in^2 and a height of 5 in. The other container is a triangular prism with a base area of 32 in^2 and a height of 6 in. Which container is the better deal? Explain.

_____

_____

7. **Critical Thinking** Can rectangular prisms have different heights and the same volume? Show your work below.

UNIT 5

Problem Solving Connections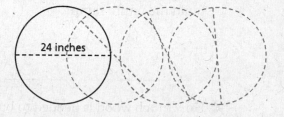

Ramp Up! Carl and Jackie plan to build two different bike ramps. They have two plans and have researched the cost of materials. They want to calculate how much the materials for both ramps will cost.

COMMON CORE

CC.7.G.4,
CC.7.G.6

1 The Plans

A The ramp will be long enough for a bike tire shown at right to rotate almost one full time. How long will the ramp be? Use 3.14 for π, and round to the nearest inch. Show your work below.

24 inches

B The ramp will be one-third as wide as it is long. How wide will it be? How did your find your answer?

_____

C Jackie's dad has a piece of wood that is 2,000 square inches. Is this enough wood to make the flat surface of the ramp they are planning? How much wood will they need just to make the flat surface of the ramp? What is one reason the piece of wood might not work?

_____

_____

_____

D On the ramp, they plan to place a circular logo that has the same size as the bike tire. How much of the ramp will the logo cover? Use 3.14 for π. Show your work below.

2 Building Ramp 1

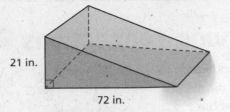

21 in.

72 in.

In the design, the ramp is a triangular prism. The height of the ramp is 21 inches, and the base measures 72 inches.

A Label the dimensions you found in **1** on the design.

B What formula could you use to calculate the amount of wood needed to build the entire ramp?

_____

_____

C How much wood is needed to build the entire ramp? Show your work below.

D Find the surface area of the ramp to the nearest square foot. *Hint:* Divide the number of square inches by 144.

_____

E To provide support for the ramp, Carl and Jackie fill the ramp with sand. Find the volume of sand in cubic inches that they used. Show your work below.

F What formula did you use to calculate the volume?

_____

G What is the volume of the ramp to the nearest cubic foot? *Hint:* Divide the number of cubic inches by 1,728.

_____

3 Building Ramp 2

For the second ramp, Carl and Jackie will need to duplicate the first ramp two times and build a rectangular prism to connect the ramps together. They sketch a side view with the dimensions.

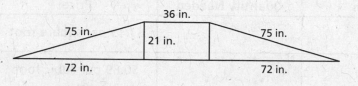

A What shape do these three figures form when combined?

_____

B How much wood is needed to build the entire ramp if they build each complete piece separately? Show your work below.

C What is the surface area to the nearest square foot? *Hint:* Divide the number of square inches by 144.

_____

D Once put together, what part of the pieces overlap, and therefore, can be subtracted from the surface area when Carl and Jackie paint it?

_____

_____

E What is the surface area of the ramp that will be painted?

_____

F Describe two ways to find the volume of this new ramp.

_____

_____

G How much sand, to the nearest cubic foot, would be needed to fill this ramp?

_____

4 Answer the Question

A   Complete the tables below to calculate the cost for each ramp.

Ramp 1			
Item	Quantity Needed	Price	Total
Wood		$1.15 per square foot	
Sand		$0.89 per cubic foot	
Paint (1 can = 300 square feet)		$22.00 per can	

Ramp 2			
Item	Quantity Needed	Price	Total
Wood		$1.15 per square foot	
Sand		$0.89 per cubic foot	
Paint (1 can = 300 square feet)		$22.00 per can	

B   What is the total cost for wood for the two ramps? _____

C   What is the total cost for sand for the two ramps? _____

D   What is the total cost paint for the two ramps? Explain your answer.

_____

_____

_____

E   How much will the materials cost Carl and Jackie to build both ramps?

_____

F   Design your own ramp and research prices online or at your neighborhood hardware store. Using the cost of the materials, calculate how much it would cost to make your ramp design.

Name _____ Class _____ Date _____

MULTIPLE CHOICE

1. Flora is drawing a pattern for a mosaic. What is the area of the pattern?

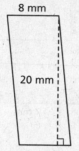

8 mm

20 mm

A. 28 square millimeters

B. 140 square millimeters

C. 160 square millimeters

D. 200 square millimeters

2. Ned forms a larger cube from centimeter cubes. What is the surface area of the larger cube?

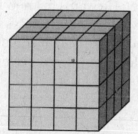

F. 90 square centimeters

G. 96 square centimeters

H. 108 square centimeters

J. 216 square centimeters

3. Maria is wrapping a present for her best friend. How much wrapping paper will she use, not counting overlap?

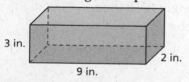

3 in.

2 in.

9 in.

A. 51 square inches

B. 54 square inches

C. 84 square inches

D. 102 square inches

4. Roberto purchases a small toy chest for his children. What is the volume of the toy chest?

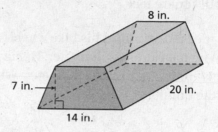

8 in.

7 in.

20 in.

14 in.

F. 1,120 cubic inches

G. 1,540 cubic inches

H. 1,960 cubic inches

J. 3,080 cubic inches

5. Carol wants to tile her utility room. Each tile is 1 square foot. She draws the shape of her room on a grid. Each square unit on the grid represents 1 square foot. How many tiles will she need?

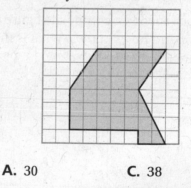

A. 30   **C.** 38

B. 34   **D.** 42

6. A circular mirror has a radius of 6 inches. What is the circumference of the mirror?

F. 3π inches

G. 6π inches

H. 12π inches

J. 36π inches

7. Michael plants a circular garden with a diameter of 10 feet. What is the area of his garden? Use 3.14 for π.

A. 31.4 square feet

B. 62.8 square feet

C. 78.5 square feet

D. 314 square feet

8. Lyle measures around his bike wheel. Then he measures its diameter. He divides the circumference by the diameter. What was the quotient?

F. 1   **H.** 3

G. 2   **J.** π

9. A circular quilt is made from 113.04 square feet of fabric. How much trim is needed to go around its edge? Use 3.14 for π.

A. 6 feet

B. 12 feet

C. 18.84 feet

D. 37.68 feet

10. An outdoor shed is a composite figure that has a floor and no windows. What is the surface area of the shed?

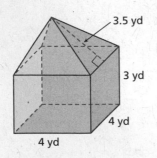

3.5 yd

3 yd

4 yd

4 yd

F. 24 square yards

G. 48 square yards

H. 76 square yards

J. 92 square yards

11. Patrick made a plastic model of his office building. He plans to paint the entire model. Use the model to find the surface area that Patrick will paint. Explain how you found this area.

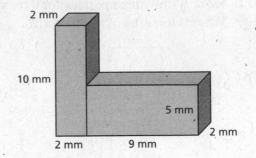

2 mm

10 mm

5 mm

2 mm

2 mm   9 mm

_____

_____

_____

_____

_____

12. Paul's circular table has a circumference of 50.24 feet. He wants to know if he should buy tablecloth that says it will cover a circular table that is 200 square feet. Should he buy the tablecloth? Explain. Use 3.14 for π.

_____

_____

_____

_____

13. Mary is filling a jar shaped like a square prism with a bag of confetti that is labeled as containing 100 cubic inches. The base of her prism is 3 inches by 3 inches and the height is 10 inches. Will all the confetti fit in the jar? Explain.

_____

_____

_____

_____

_____

Statistics and Probability: Populations and Sampling

Unit Focus

You have previously worked with populations. You found measures of center and measures of variation. When a population is large, you may only have a sample to observe and use to obtain data. You will learn how to be sure that your sample is random, not biased. You will also learn how to make sure that your data represents the entire population. You will also expand upon your understanding of population summaries by using dot plots, mean, and mean absolute deviations to compare populations.

Unit at a Glance

COMMON CORE

Lesson	Standards for Mathematical Content
6-1 Populations and Samples	CC.7.SP.1, CC.7.SP.2
6-2 Generating Multiple Samples	CC.7.SP.2
6-3 Comparing Populations	CC.7.SP.3, CC.7.SP.4
Problem Solving Connections	
Test Prep	

Unpacking the Common Core State Standards

Use the table to help you understand the Standards for Mathematical Content that are taught in this unit. Refer to the lessons listed after each standard for exploration and practice.

COMMON CORE Standards for Mathematical Content	What It Means For You
CC.7.SP.1 Understand that statistics can be used to gain information about a population by examining a sample of the population; generalizations about a population from a sample are valid only if the sample is representative of that population. Understand that random sampling tends to produce representative samples and support valid inferences. Lesson 6-1	You will learn that sampling can be misleading, particularly after a biased survey. You will determine how to complete a random survey so that your results more accurately reflect the entire population.
CC.7.SP.2 Use data from a random sample to draw inferences about a population with an unknown characteristic of interest. Generate multiple samples (or simulated samples) of the same size to gauge the variation in estimates or predictions. Lessons 6-1, 6-2	You will use the data you collect from random samples to analyze a population. You'll use a variety of techniques, including graphing calculators, to ensure randomness. You will also use multiple samples to determine how samples vary.
CC.7.SP.3 Informally assess the degree of visual overlap of two numerical data distributions with similar variabilities, measuring the difference between the centers by expressing it as a multiple of a measure of variability. Lesson 6-3	You will use the mean absolute deviation and a measure of center to compare two data sets and note their separation. You will use dot plots to visually represent this.
CC.7.SP.4 Use measures of center and measures of variability for numerical data from random samples to draw informal comparative inferences about two populations. Lesson 6-3	You will use measures of center and variability to help describe different populations. You can also make comparisons between two populations using these measures.

Populations and Samples

Essential question: *How can you use a sample to gain information about a population?*

1 EXPLORE Random and Non-Random Sampling

A vegetable garden has 100 tomato plants arranged in a 10-by-10 array. The gardener wants to know the average number of tomatoes on the plants. Each cell in the table below represents a plant. The number in the cell tells how many tomatoes are on that particular plant.

12	18	18	14	20	11	15	9	12	10
59	65	77	40	33	56	66	51	88	50
56	56	44	75	44	77	56	60	53	72
44	62	67	57	41	63	44	33	64	65
75	75	57	60	76	67	56	78	55	44
71	47	76	63	57	67	63	46	54	55
66	71	75	76	44	70	44	67	65	62
73	58	66	75	67	78	61	43	56	55
65	74	81	60	74	37	78	88	22	45
49	54	79	83	75	76	38	78	48	56

Because counting the number of tomatoes on all of the plants is too time-consuming, the gardener decides to choose 10 plants at random to find the average number of tomatoes on them.

To simulate the random selection, place this page on the floor. Drop 10 small objects onto the chart. Use these numbers for the 10 random plants.

A What is the average number of tomatoes on the 10 plants that were randomly selected?

_____

B Alternately, the gardener decides to choose the 10 plants in the first row. What is the average number of tomatoes on these 10 plants?

_____

1a. How do the averages you got with each sampling method compare?

_____

_____

1b. How do the averages you got with each sampling method compare to the average for the entire population, which is 56.3?

_____

_____

1c. Why do you think the first method gave a closer average than the second method?

_____

_____

When information is being gathered about a group, the entire group of objects, individuals, or events is called the **population**. A **sample** is part of the population chosen to represent the entire group.

A sample in which every person, object, or event has an equal chance at being selected is called a **random sample**. A random sample is more likely to be representative of the entire population than other sampling methods.

When a sample does not accurately represent the population, it is called a **biased sample**.

Use ❶ to answer the following questions.

What is the population?   What is the sample?
the farmer or the tomato plants   10 tomato plants or 100 tomato plants

Which method of sampling is a random sampling?

_____

Which method of sampling could be a biased sampling?

_____

2 EXAMPLE Identifying Samples

Determine whether each sample is a random sample or a biased sample. Explain your reasoning.

A Roberto wants to know the favorite sport of adults in his hometown. He surveys 50 adults at a baseball game.

_____

_____

B Paula wants to know the favorite type of music for students at her school. She surveys the first 60 people who enter the school doors in the morning.

_____

_____

2. You want to know which radio station people in your neighborhood listen to the most. How would you get a random sample?

_____

_____

When you have a random sample, it is representative of the population. You can use the data about the sample and proportional reasoning to make inferences or predictions about the population.

3 **EXAMPLE** **Making Predictions**

A shipment to a warehouse consists of 3,500 MP3 players. The manager chooses a random sample of 50 MP3 players and finds that 3 are defective. How many MP3 players in the shipment are likely to be defective?

A It is reasonable to make a prediction about the population because this sample is _____.

B Determine what percentage of the sample is damaged.

$\frac{3}{50} = \frac{}{100}$, so _____ % of the MP3s are damaged.

C Find 6% of the population, which is 6% of _____.

$\boxed{} \times \boxed{} = \boxed{}$

D You could also set up a proportion to make a prediction.

$$\frac{\text{defective MP3s in sample}}{\text{size of sample}} = \frac{\text{defective MP3s in population}}{\text{size of population}}$$

$$\frac{3}{50} = \frac{}{3,500}$$

Based on the sample, you can predict that _____ MP3s in the shipment would be defective.

3a. What If? How many damaged MP3 players in the shipment would you predict to be damaged if 6 MP3s in the sample had been damaged?

_____

REFLECT

3b. How could you use estimation as a way to see if your answer is reasonable?

_____

_____

PRACTICE

1. Paul and his friends average their test grades and find that the average is 95. The teacher announces that the average grade of all of her classes is 83. Why are the averages so different?

_____

_____

_____

2. Nancy hears a report that the average price of gasoline is $2.82. She averages the prices of stations near her home. She finds the average price of gas to be $3.03. Why are the averages different?

_____

_____

_____

Determine whether each sample is a random sample or a biased sample. Explain your reasoning.

3. Carol wants to find out the favorite foods of students at her middle school. She asks the boys' basketball team about their favorite foods.

_____

_____

_____

4. Dallas wants to know what elective subjects the students at his school like best. He surveys students who are leaving band class.

_____

_____

_____

5. A manager samples the receipts of every fifth person who goes through the line. Out of 50 people, 4 had a mispriced item. If 600 people go to this store each day, how many people would you expect to have a mispriced item?

_____

6. Jerry randomly selects 20 boxes of crayons from the shelf and finds 2 boxes with at least one broken crayon. If the shelf holds 130 boxes, how many would you expect to have at least one broken crayon?

_____

Generating Multiple Samples

COMMON CORE

CC.7.SP.2

Essential question: *How can you use samples to make and compare predictions about a population?*

A store gets a shipment of 1,000 light bulbs, 200 of which are defective upon arrival. The store's manager does not know this. She wants to predict the number of defective light bulbs by testing a sample of the shipment.

1 EXPLORE Generating a Small Sample

A The manager will want to use a random sample to represent the entire shipment. One way to simulate a random sample is to use a graphing calculator to generate random integers.

To simulate picking out random light bulbs between 1 and 1,000:

- Press MATH , scroll right and select **PRB**, then select **5: randInt(**.

- Enter the smallest value, comma, largest possible value.

- Hit ENTER to generate random numbers.

In this specific case, you will enter **randInt(** ___ , ___ **)** because there are _____ light bulbs in the shipment.

The numbers that are generated will each represent bulbs in the shipment.

Let numbers 1 to 200 represent bulbs that are _____.

Numbers 201 to 1,000 will represent bulbs that are _____.

Generate four numbers and record your results in the table below.

Random Sample of Light Bulbs		
Bulb	**Random Number Generated**	**Defective or Working?**
1		
2		
3		
4		

B Based on this sample, how many defective light bulbs should the manager expect to find in the shipment?

_____

_____

1. You and your classmates have generated multiple samples. Compare your results to those of your classmates. How do your predictions compare?

_____

_____

Generating a Larger Sample

A   Repeat the process. This time, collect a sample of 20 light bulbs.

On a separate sheet of paper copy the table from **1** and record your results in the table.

B   Based on this sample, how many defective light bulbs should the manager expect to find in the shipment?

_____

2a. You and your classmates have generated multiple samples. Compare your results to those of your classmates. How do your predictions compare?

_____

_____

2b. The _____ the sample size, the _____ the variability. Thus larger samples give _____ results.

2c. Estimate the average number of pets per household for your schoolmates. Explain your sampling process and estimate.

_____

_____

_____

2d. Compare your estimate of the average number of pets per household with those of your classmates.

_____

_____

Comparing Populations

Essential question: *How can you use measures of center and variability to compare two populations?*

COMMON CORE

CC.7.SP.3
CC.7.SP.4

1 EXPLORE **Analyzing Dot Plots**

The school nurse measured all of the boys' heights during their physical education class. She made a list of the basketball players' heights and the soccer players' heights.

Basketball Players' Heights (in.)
69, 70, 72, 73, 73, 73, 74, 75, 75, 76

Soccer Players' Heights (in.)
65, 66, 68, 69, 69, 70, 70, 70, 71, 72

A Make a dot plot of the heights of the basketball players.

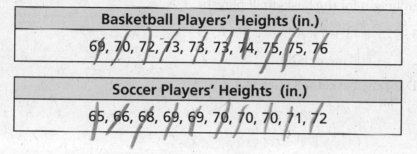

B Make a dot plot of the heights of the soccer players.

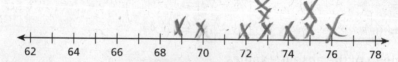

REFLECT

1. What can you conclude about the data sets based on your plots?

   Most of the heights in inches are in the 70s.

   The data sets have a similar ___*rang*___, but the basketball data are ___*placed*___ to the right.

Dot plots are useful for informally comparing data sets. However, it is also helpful to calculate measures of center and measures of variability.

Recall that one measure of center is the mean. To find the mean, you add the data points and then divide the sum by the number of data points in the set.

To find the mean absolute deviation (MAD):

- Find the mean of the data.
- Take the absolute value of the difference between the mean and each data point.
- Then find the mean of those absolute values.

2 EXPLORE **Calculating Measures of Center and Variability**

Use the data sets from **1**.

A Calculate the mean height for the basketball players.

$69 + 70 + 72 + 73 + 73 + 73 + 74 + 75 + 75 + 76 =$ ☐

☐ $\div 10 =$ ☐   The mean is _____.

B Calculate the MAD for the basketball players.

$|69 - 73| =$ ☐ $|73 - 73| =$ ☐
$|70 - 73| =$ ☐ $|74 - 73| =$ ☐
$|72 - 73| =$ ☐ $|75 - 73| =$ ☐
$|73 - 73| =$ ☐ $|75 - 73| =$ ☐
$|73 - 73| =$ ☐ $|76 - 73| =$ ☐

Find the mean of the absolute values.

☐ + ☐ + ☐ + ☐ + ☐ + ☐ + ☐ + ☐ + ☐ + ☐ = ☐

☐ $\div 10 =$ ☐   The MAD is _____.

C Calculate the mean height for the soccer players.

$65 + 66 + 68 + 69 + 69 + 70 + 70 + 70 + 71 + 72 =$ ☐

☐ $\div 10 =$ ☐   The mean is _____.

D Calculate the MAD for the soccer players.

$|65 - 69| =$ ☐ $|70 - 69| =$ ☐
$|66 - 69| =$ ☐ $|70 - 69| =$ ☐
$|68 - 69| =$ ☐ $|70 - 69| =$ ☐
$|69 - 69| =$ ☐ $|71 - 69| =$ ☐
$|69 - 69| =$ ☐ $|72 - 69| =$ ☐

Find the mean of the absolute values.

☐ + ☐ + ☐ + ☐ + ☐ + ☐ + ☐ + ☐ + ☐ + ☐ = ☐

☐ $\div 10 =$ ☐   The MAD is _____.

E How are the mean and the MAD reflected in the dot plots?

_____

_____

F Find the difference in the means.

$73 - 69 =$ ☐

G Write the difference of means as a multiple of the MAD.

$4 = 1.6 \times$ ☐

The means of the two data sets differ by _____ times the amount that an individual height varies.

REFLECT

2. If two data sets have the same mean but different MADs, how would that reflect in the dot plot?

_____

_____

In **1** and **2**, we had the data for an entire population. Sometimes, it is only possible to get a sample of a population, but you can still use similar ideas to make comparisons about the populations using these samples.

3 **EXPLORE** **Comparing Large Populations**

Paula and Dean wanted to determine the average word length in two books. They took a random sample of 12 words each and counted the length of each word from each book.

Book 1 Word Count
3, 7, 5, 2, 4, 3, 1, 6, 4, 8, 2, 3

Book 2 Word Count
5, 4, 3, 6, 4, 5, 5, 2, 3, 4, 2, 5

A Calculate the mean for Book 1. Show your work below.

B Calculate the MAD for Book 1. _____

C Calculate the mean for Book 2. Show your work below.

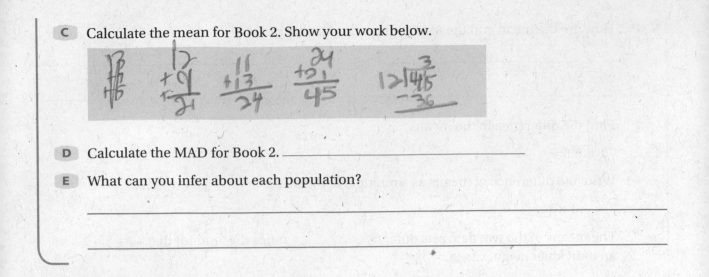

D Calculate the MAD for Book 2. _____

E What can you infer about each population?

_____

_____

PRACTICE

Carol wants to know how many people live in each household in her town. She conducts two random surveys of 10 people each and asks how many people live in their home. Her results are listed below. Use the data for 1–6.

Sample A: 1, 6, 2, 4, 4, 3, 5, 5, 2, 8

Sample B: 3, 4, 5, 4, 3, 2, 4, 5, 4, 4

1. Make a dot plot for Sample A.

2. Make a dot plot for Sample B.

3. Find the mean and MAD for Sample A.

Mean: 40

MAD: _____

4. Find the mean and MAD for Sample B.

Mean: 3.8

MAD: _____

5. What can you infer about the population based on Sample A? Explain.

The population is very small population

6. What can you infer about the population based on Sample B? Explain.

The population is not really high.

Problem Solving Connections

Happy Birthday! Abby is planning a big birthday party. She has invited everyone in her grade and has sent 80 invitations. Unfortunately, she forgot to include an RSVP on the invitation, and she wants to know how many people are coming to the party. On the invitation, Abby requested no gifts. Instead, she is asking everyone to make a donation to her favorite charity.

How much money can Abby make for her charity at her birthday party?

COMMON CORE

CC.7.SP.1,
CC.7.SP.2,
CC.7.SP.3,
CC.7.SP.4

1 Using a Sample to Make a Prediction

A Abby asks 10 of her closest friends, and 9 of them will be attending the party. Based on this survey, how many people should Abby expect to come to the party? Show your work below.

B Who is the population in this event?

_____

C Who is the sample in Abby's survey?

_____

D Is the sample random? Explain.

_____

_____

E Explain why Abby's sample could be biased.

_____

_____

F Do you think that Abby's results are too high or too low? Explain.

_____

_____

2 Using a Random Sample to Make a Prediction

A Why is it important for a sample to be random in order to make an accurate prediction?

_____

_____

_____

B How might Abby obtain a random sample?

_____

_____

_____

C What can Abby do to increase the accuracy of her random sample?

_____

_____

D Abby has a list of everyone in her class. She numbers all the names on the list from 1 to 80. Then, Abby uses her graphing calculator to generate 20 random numbers. She e-mails each of the people who correspond to the randomly generated numbers and asks whether or not he or she plans to attend the party. Of the 20 people surveyed, 6 are not able to come to the party. Based on this sample, predict the total number of people who will attend the party. Show your work below.

E How does this random sample provide a more accurate count of who might not attend the party than the first sample?

_____

_____

_____

F Why might this still not be an accurate prediction?

_____

_____

_____

3 Comparing Populations

The first 10 monetary donations from boys and the first 10 monetary donations from girls were recorded.

Donation Amounts from Boys ($)
15, 10, 10, 5, 12, 20, 15, 5, 10, 10

Donation Amounts from Girls ($)
10, 20, 5, 1, 20, 25, 15, 15, 10, 5

A Make a dot plot for each set of data.

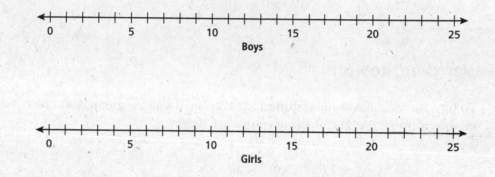

B What can you infer about the donations of each of the populations?

_____

_____

_____

C Find the mean and mean absolute deviation for the boys' donations.
Show your work below.

D Based on the data set and the line plots, how would you expect the mean and the mean absolute deviation for the girls' donations to compare?

_____

_____

E Find the mean and the mean absolute deviation for the girls' donations. Show your work below.

4 Answer the Question

A To find the average student donation, average the girls' mean donation and the boys' mean donation. Show your work below.

B Based on the mean student donation, and Abby's prediction from **2** of how many people will come to her party, how much money could be raised in donations?

C Since people generally make donations in whole dollar amounts, find the amount of money that could be raised in donations based on all the information given. Explain your reasoning and show your work below.

Name _____ Class _____ Date _____

MULTIPLE CHOICE

1. Which is a measure of center?

   A. distance

   B. mean absolute deviation

   C. mean

   D. sample

2. You want to know the favorite sport of middle school students. Which group would provide a random sample?

   F. the girls' soccer team

   G. the band

   H. every fifth person who leaves the school building at the end of the school day

   J. every tenth person who enters the stadium before a football game

3. How can you make a random sample more accurately reflect the population it represents?

   A. carefully select the data pieces

   B. increase the number of pieces of random data

   C. use a graphing calculator to provide random integers

   D. survey a biased group

4. A department store receives a shipment of 1,000 glasses. Out of a random sample of 10 glasses, 2 are broken. How many glasses would you expect to be broken in the entire shipment?

   F. 2

   G. 50

   H. 200

   J. 250

5. A random sample of a shipment of furniture shows that 2 out of 50 boxes do not contain all of the correct parts. Which proportion could help you find the number of boxes that will not contain the correct parts out of a shipment of 500?

   A. $\frac{2}{50} = \frac{500}{x}$ C. $\frac{50}{500} = \frac{x}{2}$

   B. $\frac{x}{50} = \frac{500}{2}$ D. $\frac{2}{50} = \frac{x}{500}$

6. A restaurant manager predicts that out of the 200 people that will come to the restaurant in one day, 40 people will order dessert. He based this on a random sample of people he polled yesterday. What ratio could his prediction be based on?

   F. $\frac{1}{5}$ H. $\frac{10}{25}$

   G. $\frac{7}{10}$ J. $\frac{2}{50}$

7. Maria collects data about the scores on a math test. She finds that the test has a low mean absolute deviation. Which dot plot could represent this data?

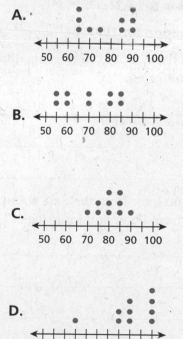

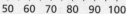

8. What does the mean absolute deviation tell you?

  F. the average of the data

  G. where the data is centered on a number line

  H. how many dots are above each value on a dot plot

  J. how far the data is spread out from the mean

9. A teacher randomly reads 10 one-page reports written by her students. She finds that 3 of the reports have misspellings. How many reports would she expect to have misspellings if she reads 150 reports?

  A. 10   **B.** 45

  C. 50   **D.** 100

FREE RESPONSE

Peter records the monthly high temperatures, in degrees Fahrenheit at his house for a year. He calculates the mean to be 63 and the mean absolute deviation to be 4.67.

Jorge records the monthly high temperatures, in degrees Fahrenheit at his house for a year. He calculates the mean to be 63 and the mean absolute deviation to be 21.67.

Use this information for 10–11.

10. How would the dot plots of the data differ for Peter and Jorge?

_____

_____

_____

11. What can you infer from the data about the areas where Peter and Jorge live?

_____

_____

_____

12. Explain why surveying 100 different people from the phone book might not be a random sample.

_____

_____

_____

13. A factory produces 500,000 nails per day. The manager of the factory estimates that there are less than 1,500 misshapen nails made per day. A random survey of 500 nails finds 4 misshapen ones. Is the manager correct in his estimate? Explain.

_____

_____

_____

_____

Jane reports the number of years she has known each person in her close group of friends: 5, 8, 4, 2, 9, 10, 3, 11

Jack reports the same information for his group of friends: 4, 2, 3, 1, 4, 3, 5, 2

Use the data for 14–16.

14. Find the mean and mean absolute value for both Jane's data and Jack's data.

_____

_____

15. How would you expect the data sets' dot plots to compare to each other?

_____

_____

_____

16. What can you infer about both groups of friends?

_____

_____

_____

Probability and Simulations

Unit Focus

In this unit, you will learn about probability. You will learn how to express the likelihood of something occurring. You will learn the definitions of an experiment, a trial, an outcome, and an event. You will calculate the experimental probability of an event and compare that number to its theoretical probability. You will make predictions based on probability. You will also learn about compound probability and different ways to find its value. Additionally, you will conduct simulations using a random number generator on a graphing calculator.

Unit at a Glance

COMMON CORE

Lesson	Standards for Mathematical Content
7-1 Understanding Probability	CC.7.SP.5
7-2 Theoretical Probability	CC.7.SP.6, CC.7.SP.7a
7-3 Experimental Probability	CC.7.SP.6, CC.7.SP.7a, CC.7.SP.7b
7-4 Compound Events	CC.7.SP.8a, CC.7.SP.8b
7-5 Conducting a Simulation	CC.7.SP.8c
Problem Solving Connections	
Test Prep	

Unpacking the Common Core State Standards

Use the table to help you understand the Standards for Mathematical Content that are taught in this unit. Refer to the lessons listed after each standard for exploration and practice.

COMMON CORE Standards for Mathematical Content	What It Means For You
CC.7.SP.5 Understand that the probability of a chance event is a number between 0 and 1 that expresses the likelihood of the event occurring. Larger numbers indicate greater likelihood. A probability near 0 indicates an unlikely event, a probability around 1/2 indicates an event that is neither unlikely nor likely, and a probability near 1 indicates a likely event. Lesson 7-1	You will describe the likelihood of an event using words and numbers from 0 to 1. You will find the probability of an event and its complement.
CC.7.SP.6 Approximate the probability of a chance event by collecting data on the chance process that produces it and observing its long-run relative frequency, and predict the approximate relative frequency given the probability. Lessons 7-2, 7-3	You will calculate theoretical and experimental probabilities and compare the experimental probability to the theoretical probability.
CC.7.SP.7a Develop a uniform probability model by assigning equal probability to all outcomes, and use the model to determine probabilities of events. Lessons 7-2, 7-3	You will work with ratios that represent the theoretical probabilities of events.
CC.7.SP.7b Develop a probability model (which may not be uniform) by observing frequencies in data generated from a chance process. Lesson 7-3	You will use real-life observations to find the experimental probability of an event.
CC.7.SP.8a Understand that, just as with simple events, the probability of a compound event is the fraction of outcomes in the sample space for which the compound event occurs. Lesson 7-4	You will find all the outcomes in the sample space of a compound event. Then using that sample space you will find the probability of the compound event.
CC.7.SP.8b Represent sample spaces for compound events using methods such as organized lists, tables and tree diagrams. For an event described in everyday language (e.g., "rolling double sixes"), identify the outcomes in the sample space which compose the event. Lesson 7-4	You will find all possible outcomes for a sample space and you will find those outcomes that make up a compound event.
CC.7.SP.8c Design and use a simulation to generate frequencies for compound events. Lesson 7-5	You will conduct trials of an experiment using a random number generator.

Understanding Probability

Essential question: *How can you describe the likelihood of an event?*

COMMON CORE

CC.7.SP.5

1 EXPLORE   Likelihood of an Event

When a number cube is rolled once, the possible
numbers that could show face up are _____.

Each time you roll the cube, a number lands face up. This is called an *event*.
Below is a list of 9 different events.

Work with a partner to order the events from those least likely to happen to the
ones that are most likely to happen when you roll the number cube one time.

Use the space next to each event to write any notes that might help you
order them.

Rolling a number less than 7 _____

Rolling an 8 _____

Rolling a 1, 2, or 3 _____

Rolling a 5 _____

Rolling a number other than 6 _____

Rolling an even number _____

Rolling a number greater than 5 _____

Rolling an odd number _____

Rolling a prime number _____

The order I wrote the events in is:

_____

_____

_____

REFLECT

1a. How did you sort the events?

_____

_____

_____

1b. Are any of the events impossible?

_____

_____

An **experiment** is an activity involving chance in which results are observed. Each observation of an experiment is a **trial**, and each result is an **outcome**. A set of one or more outcomes is an **event**.

The **probability** of an event, written P(event), measures the likelihood that the event will occur. Probability is a measure between 0 and 1 as shown on the number line and can be written as a fraction, a decimal, or percent.

If the event is not likely to occur very many times, the probability of the event is close to 0. Likewise, if an event is likely to occur many times, the event's probability is closer to 1.

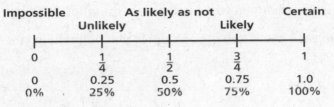

2 **EXAMPLE** Describing Events

Determine whether each event is impossible, unlikely, as likely as not, likely, or certain. Then, tell whether the probability is 0, close to 0, $\frac{1}{2}$, close to 1, or 1.

A   You flip a coin. The coin lands heads up.

_____

B   You roll two number cubes and the sum of the numbers is 10.

_____

C   A bowl contains 14 red marbles and 3 green marbles. You pick a red marble.

_____

D   A spinner has 10 equal sections marked 1 through 10. You spin and land on a number greater than 0.

_____

TRY THIS!

Describe each event as impossible, unlikely, as likely as not, likely, or certain. Tell whether the probability is 0, close to 0, $\frac{1}{2}$, close to 1, or 1.

2a. A hat contains pieces of paper marked with the numbers 1 through 16. You pick an even number.

2b. A spinner has 6 equal sections marked 1 through 6. You spin and land on 0.

_____   _____

2c. The probability of event A is $\frac{1}{3}$. The probability of event B is $\frac{1}{4}$. What can you conclude about the two events?

_____

_____

The **complement** of an event is the set of all outcomes *not* included in the event. For example, consider the event that you roll a number cube and get a 3. The complement is the event that you do not roll a 3. The complement is rolling a 1, 2, 4, 5, or 6.

The sum of the probabilities of an event and its complement equals 1.

$$P(\text{event}) + P(\text{complement}) = 1$$

3 EXAMPLE Using the Complement of an Event

In a standard deck of cards, the probability of choosing a card at random and getting an ace is $\frac{1}{13}$. What is the probability of not getting an ace?

$P(\text{event}) + P(\text{complement}) = $ _____

$P(\text{ace}) + P($ _____ $) = 1$

_____ $+ P($ _____ $) = 1$

$P(\text{not getting an ace}) = 1 - \dfrac{}{}$

$= \dfrac{}{}$

TRY THIS!

3a. A jar contains balls marked with the numbers 1 through 8. The probability that you pick a number at random and get a 5 is $\frac{1}{8}$. What is the probability of not picking a 5?

_____

3b. You roll a number cube. The probability that you roll an even number is $\frac{1}{2}$. What is the probability you will roll an odd number?

_____

REFLECT

3c. Why do the probability of an event and the probability of its complement add up to 1?

_____

_____

_____

_____

3d. Give an example of a real-world event and its complement.

_____

_____

_____

PRACTICE

1. In a hat, you have index cards with the numbers 1 through 10 written on them. You pick one card at random. Order the events from least likely to happen to most likely to happen.

   You pick a number greater than 0.   You pick a number that is at least 2.

   You pick an even number.   You pick a number that is at most 0.

   _____

   _____

Determine whether each event is impossible, unlikely, as likely as not, likely, or certain. Then, tell whether the probability is 0, close to 0, $\frac{1}{2}$, close to 1, or 1.

2. randomly picking a green card from a standard deck of playing cards

   _____

3. randomly picking a red card from a standard deck of playing cards

   _____

4. picking a number less that 15 from a jar with papers labeled from 1 to 12

   _____

5. picking a number that is divisible by 5 from a jar with papers labeled from 1 to 12

   _____

6. The probability of rolling a 5 on a number cube is $\frac{1}{6}$. What is the probability of not rolling a 5? _____

7. The probability that a coin will land heads when flipping a coin is $\frac{1}{2}$. What is the probability of getting tails? _____

8. The probability of spinning a 4 on a spinner with 5 equal sections marked 1 through 5 is $\frac{1}{5}$. What is the probability of not landing on 4? _____

9. The probability of picking a queen from a standard deck of cards is $\frac{1}{13}$. What is the probability of not picking a queen? _____

10. Describe an event that has a probability of 0% and an event that has a probability of 100%.

   _____

   _____

Theoretical Probability

Essential question: *How can you find the theoretical probability of an event?*

COMMON
CORE

CC.7.SP.6
CC.7.SP.7a

1 EXPLORE Finding Theoretical Probability

At a school fair, you have a choice of spinning Spinner A or
Spinner B. You win a MP3 player if the spinner lands on a section
with a star in it. Which spinner should you choose if you want
the best chance of winning?

Complete the table.

Spinner A

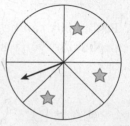

	Spinner A	Spinner B
Total Number of Outcomes		
Number of Sections with Stars		
P(winning MP3) $=$ $\frac{\text{Number of sections with stars}}{\text{Total number of outcomes}}$		

Spinner B

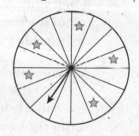

Compare the ratios for Spinner A and Spinner B.

The ratio for Spinner _____ is greater than the ratio for Spinner _____.

I should choose _____ for the best chance of winning.

REFLECT

1a. *Theoretical probability* is a way to describe how you found the chance of
winning a MP3 player in the scenario above. Using the spinner example to help
you, explain in your own words how to find the theoretical probability of an event.

_____

_____

_____

1b. Suppose you choose Spinner A. What is the probability that you will not win? Show
your work below.

1c. **What If?** If you could change something about Spinner B, what could make your chances of winning equal to your chances of not winning? Explain.

_____

_____

Theoretical probability is the probability that an event occurs when all of the outcomes of the experiment are equally likely.

> ### Theoretical Probability
>
> $$P(\text{event}) = \frac{\text{number of ways the event can occur}}{\text{total number of equally likely outcomes}}$$

Probability can be written as a fraction, a decimal, or a percent. For example, the probability you win with Spinner B is $\frac{5}{16}$. You can also write that as 0.3125 or as 31.25%.

2 EXAMPLE Calculating Theoretical Probability

A A bag contains 8 red marbles and 12 green marbles. You choose one marble out of the bag without looking. What is the probability that you choose a red marble? Write your answer in simplest form.

$$P(\text{red marble}) = \frac{\text{number of red marbles}}{\text{total number of marbles in the bag}} = \frac{\quad}{\quad} = \underline{\quad}$$

B You roll a number cube one time. What is the probability that you roll a 3 or 4? Write your answer in simplest form.

$$P(\text{rolling a 3 or 4}) = \frac{\qquad\qquad}{\qquad\qquad} = \frac{\quad}{\quad} = \underline{\quad}$$

TRY THIS!

Find the probability of each event. Write your answer in simplest form.

2a. A spinner has 3 equally-sized sections— one is green, one is yellow, and one is blue. You spin the spinner once. What is the probability that the spinner lands on blue?

_____

2b. You pick at random one card from a standard deck of playing cards. What is the probability that you pick a black card?

_____

REFLECT

2c. Describe a situation that has a theoretical probability of $\frac{1}{4}$?

_____

_____

Probability can be used to make predictions. If the theoretical probability of an event is $\frac{1}{3}$, you expect it to happen about $\frac{1}{3}$ of the time. When performing multiple trials, you can use probability to predict the number of times the outcome should theoretically occur.

3 EXAMPLE Making a Prediction

A If you roll a number cube 600 times, about how many times do you expect to roll a 3 or a 6?

Step 1: Find the probability of the event. Write your answer in simplest form.

$$P(\text{rolling a 3 or 6}) = \frac{\rule{4cm}{0.4cm}}{\rule{4cm}{0.4cm}} = \frac{}{} = \frac{}{}$$

Step 2: Predict the number of times you will roll a 3 or a 6 in 600 trials. Multiply the probability of the event by 600.

$$\frac{}{} \times 600 = \boxed{}$$

You can expect to roll a 3 or a 6 about _____ times out of 600.

B A spinner has six sections of equal size. Two sections are colored blue, 3 sections are colored red, and 1 section is colored yellow. If you spin the spinner 50 times, how often do you expect to land on blue?

Step 1: Find the probability of the event. Write your answer in simplest form.

$$P(\text{blue}) = \frac{}{} = \frac{}{}$$

Step 2: Predict the number of times the spinner will land on blue in 50 trials. Multiply the probability of the event by 50.

$$\frac{}{} \times 50 = \frac{}{} = \boxed{}\frac{}{}$$

Since the fraction is greater than $\frac{1}{2}$, round the mixed number to the nearest whole number.

You can predict that the spinner will land on blue about _____ times out of 50 spins.

REFLECT

3. Look back to your answer in **A** . Do you think your answer means you will definitely roll a 3 or a 6 exactly the amount given by your answer?

_____

_____

_____

PRACTICE

At a school fair, you have a choice of randomly picking a ball from Basket A or Basket B. Basket A has 5 green balls, 3 red balls, and 8 yellow balls. Basket B has 7 green balls, 4 red balls, and 9 yellow balls. You can win a digital book reader if you pick a red ball.

	Basket A	Basket B
Total Number of Outcomes		
Number of Red Balls		
P(win) = $\frac{\text{Number of red balls}}{\text{Total number of outcomes}}$		

1. Complete the chart. Write each answer in simplest form.

2. Which basket should you choose if you want the better chance of winning?

_____

3. Jim has 4 nickels, 6 pennies, 4 dimes and 2 quarters in his pocket. He picks a coin at random. What is the probability that he will pick a nickel or a dime? Write your answer as a fraction, as a decimal, and as a percent.

_____

4. A class has 12 boys and 15 girls. The teacher randomly picks one child to lead the class in singing.

   a. What is the probability that the teacher picks a boy? _____

   b. What is the probability that the teacher picks a girl? _____

   c. Describe two different ways you could find the answer to part b.

   _____

   _____

Use the spinner for 5–8.

5. In 20 spins, about how often can you expect to land on a number evenly divisible by 2? _____

6. In 150 spins, about how often can you expect to land on a number less than 6? _____

7. In 200 spins, about how often can you expect to land on a 1? _____

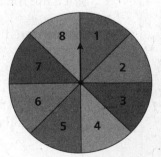

8. **Error Analysis** Rudolfo says there is a greater chance of landing on an even number than on an odd number. What is his error?

_____

_____

Experimental Probability

Essential question: *How do you find the experimental probability of an event?*

COMMON
CORE

CC.7.SP.6
CC.7.SP.7a
CC.7.SP.7b

1 EXPLORE Finding Experimental Probability

You can toss a paper cup to demonstrate *experimental probability*.

Consider tossing a paper cup. What are the three different ways the cup could land?

_____

Toss a paper cup twenty times. Record your observations in the table.

Outcome	Number of Times
Open-end up	
Open-end down	
On its side	

REFLECT

1a. Which outcome do you think is most likely?

_____

1b. Describe the three outcomes using the words *likely* and *unlikely*.

_____

_____

1c. Use the number of times each event occurred to calculate the probability of each event.

1d. What do you think would happen if you performed more trials?

_____

_____

_____

_____

Outcome	Experimental Probability
Open-end up	$\dfrac{\text{open-end up}}{20} = \dfrac{}{20}$
Open-end down	$\dfrac{\text{open-end down}}{20} = \dfrac{}{20}$
On its side	$\dfrac{\text{on its side}}{20} = \dfrac{}{20}$

1e. What is the sum of the three probabilities in **1c**?

_____

It is sometimes impossible or inconvenient to calculate theoretical probabilities. You can use *experimental probability* to estimate the probability of an event. The **experimental probability** of the event is found by comparing the number of times the event occurs to the total number of trials.

Experimental Probability

$$probability \approx \frac{number\ of\ times\ the\ event\ occurs}{total\ number\ of\ trials}$$

2 EXAMPLE Calculating Experimental Probability

Martin has a bag of marbles. He removed one marble, recorded the color and then placed it back in the bag. He repeated this process several times and recorded his results in the table.

Color	Frequency
Red	12
Blue	10
Green	15
Yellow	13

A Number of trials = _____

B Complete the table of experimental probabilities. Write each answer in simplest form.

Color	Experimental Probability
Red	$\frac{frequency\ of\ the\ event}{total\ number\ of\ trials} = \frac{\quad}{\quad} = \frac{\quad}{\quad}$
Blue	$\frac{frequency\ of\ the\ event}{total\ number\ of\ trials} = \frac{\quad}{\quad} = \frac{\quad}{\quad}$
Green	$\frac{frequency\ of\ the\ event}{total\ number\ of\ trials} = \frac{\quad}{\quad} = \frac{\quad}{\quad}$
Yellow	$\frac{frequency\ of\ the\ event}{total\ number\ of\ trials} = \frac{\quad}{\quad}$

REFLECT

2. What are two different ways you could find the experimental probability of the event that you do not draw a red marble?

_____

_____

_____

_____

3 EXPLORE Comparing Theoretical and Experimental Probability

A You roll a number cube once. Complete the table of theoretical probabilities for the different outcomes. Remember that theoretical probability is the ratio of the number of ways an event can occur to the total number of equally likely outcomes.

Number	1	2	3	4	5	6
Theoretical Probability						

B Using your knowledge of theoretical probability, predict the number of times each number will be rolled out of 30 total rolls.

1: ___ times   3: ___ times   5: ___ times

2: ___ times   4: ___ times   6: ___ times

C Roll a number cube 30 times. Complete the table for the frequency of each number and then find its experimental probability.

Number	1	2	3	4	5	6
Frequency						
Experimental Probability						

D Look at the tables you completed. How do the experimental probabilities compare with the theoretical probabilities?

_____

_____

E **Conjecture** By performing more trials, you tend to get experimental results that are closer to the theoretical probabilities. Combine your table from **C** with those of your classmates to make one table for the class. How do the class experimental probabilities compare with the theoretical probabilities?

_____

_____

REFLECT

3. Could the experimental probabilities ever be exactly equal to the theoretical probability? Why or why not?

_____

_____

1. Toss a coin at least 20 times. Record the outcomes in the table.

2. What do you think would happen if you performed more trials?

_____

_____

Tossing of Coin	Number of Times	Experimental Probability
Heads		
Tails		

3. Sonja has a bag of ping pong balls. She removed one ball, recorded the marking and then placed it back in the bag. She repeated this process several times and recorded her results in the table. Find the experimental probability of each marked ping pong ball. Write your answers in simplest form.

Type	Frequency
Stripes	12
Polka dots	13
Stars	18
Solid color	17
Squares	10

Stripes: ☐   Polka dots: ☐

Stars: ☐   Solid color: ☐   Squares: ☐

Use a spinner with six equal sections for 4–6.

4. What is the theoretical probability of landing on a specific section of your spinner?

_____

5. Spin the spinner 30 times. Complete the table.

Color or Numbered Section						
Frequency						
Experimental Probability						

6. Look at the tables you completed. How do the experimental probabilities compare with the theoretical probabilities?

_____

_____

7. **Critical Thinking** Patricia finds that the experimental probability of her dog wanting to go outside between 4 P.M. and 5 P.M. is $\frac{7}{12}$. About what percent of the time does her dog not want to go out between 4 P.M. and 5 P.M.?

_____

_____

Compound Events

COMMON
CORE

CC.7.SP.8a
CC.7.SP.8b

Essential question: *How do you find the probability of a compound event?*

A **compound event** consists of two or more single events. To find the probability of a compound event, write a ratio of the number of ways the compound event can happen to the total number of possible outcomes. The **sample space** of an experiment is the set of all possible outcomes. To find the sample space for an experiment, you can use tables, lists, and tree diagrams.

1 EXPLORE — Using a Table with Compound Events

Jacob rolls two fair number cubes. Find the probability that the sum of the numbers he rolls is 8.

A Use the table to find the sample space for rolling a particular sum on two number cubes. Each cell is the sum of the first number in that row and column.

	1	2	3	4	5	6
1						
2						
3						
4						
5						
6						

B How many possible outcomes are in the sample space?

_____

C Circle the outcomes that give the sum of 8.

D How many ways are there to roll a sum of 8? _____

E What is the probability of rolling a sum of 8? _____

TRY THIS!

Find the probability of each event.

1a. Rolling a sum less than 5 _____

1b. Rolling a sum of 7 or a sum of 9 _____

REFLECT

1c. Give an example of an event that is more likely than rolling a sum of 8.

_____

1d. Give an example of an event that is less likely than rolling a sum of 8.

_____

A deli prepares a selection of grab-and-go sandwiches with one type of bread (white or wheat), one type of meat (ham, turkey, or chicken), and one type of cheese (cheddar or Swiss). Each combination is equally likely. Find the probability of choosing a sandwich at random and getting turkey and Swiss on wheat bread.

A Complete the tree diagram to find the sample space for the compound event.

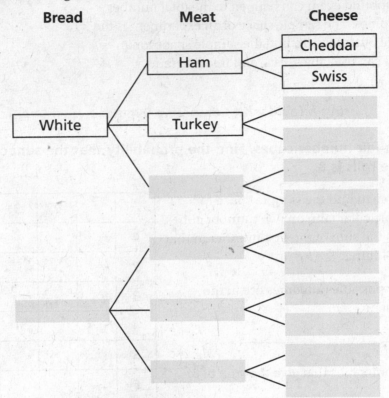

B How many possible outcomes are in the sample space? _____

C What is the probability of choosing turkey and Swiss on wheat bread at random? _____

REFLECT

2a. How can you find the probability of choosing a sandwich at random that is on wheat bread?

_____

_____

_____

2b. How can you find the probability of choosing a sandwich at random that does not have ham?

_____

_____

When a person opens a new account at Joe's bank, he or she is randomly assigned a temporary PIN. The PIN is a 3-digit security code that uses the digits 5, 6, or 7. Any of these numbers may be repeated. Find the probability that Joe's temporary PIN is 777.

Make an organized list to find the sample space.

A First list all the PINs that start with 5 and have 5 as the second digit.
Fill in the third digit with all the possibilities.

5	5	5
5	5	

B Next, list the PINs that start with 5 and have 6 as the second digit.
Fill in the third digit with all the possibilities.

5	6	
5		

C Next, list the PINs that start with 5 and have 7 as the second digit.
Fill in the third digit with all the possibilities.

5		
5		

D You have now listed all the PINs that start with 5.
Repeat **A** through **C** for PINs that start with 6.

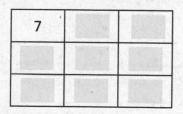

6	5	
6		

6	6	
6		

6		
6		

E Repeat **A** through **C** for PINs that start with 7.

7		

F How many possible outcomes are in the sample space? _____

G What is the probability that Joe's temporary PIN is 777? _____

REFLECT

3a. What is the probability that Joe's PIN includes at least one 5? _____

3b. What is the probability that Joe's PIN includes exactly two 6s? _____

Drake rolls two fair number cubes.

1. Complete the table to find the sample space for rolling a particular product on two number cubes.

	1	2	3	4	5	6
1						
2						
3						
4						
5						
6						

2. What is the probability that the product of the two numbers Drake rolls is a multiple of 4?

_____

3. What is the probability that the product of the two numbers Drake rolls is less than 13?

_____

Mattias gets dressed in the dark one morning and chooses his clothes at random. He chooses a shirt (green, red, or yellow), a pair of pants (black or blue), and a pair of shoes (checkered or red).

4. Use the space at right to make a tree diagram to find the sample space.

5. What is the probability that Mattias picks an outfit at random that includes red shoes?

_____

Lockers at Erin's gym have a lock with a randomly assigned three-digit code. The code uses the digits 2, 3, or 8. Any of these numbers may be repeated.

6. Use the space at right to make an organized list to find the sample space.

7. What is the probability that Erin's locker has a code with at least one 8?

_____

Conducting a Simulation

COMMON
CORE

CC.7.SP.8c

Essential question: *How can you use simulations to estimate probabilities?*

1 EXPLORE Designing and Conducting a Simulation

There are winning prize codes in 30% of a cereal company's cereal boxes. What is the probability that you have to buy at least 3 boxes of cereal to find a winning prize code?

A Design a simulation to model the situation.

Represent each box by a random number from 1 to 10. Since 30% of the boxes have a winning prize code, the numbers 1 to 3 will represent the boxes containing a winning code. The numbers 4 to 10 represent the boxes not containing a winning code.

B Conduct trials and record the results in the second column of the table.

For each trial, use a random number generator on a graphing calculator to generate a random integer from 1 to 10. Continue generating random numbers until you get a number from 1 to 3 (representing a winning code). Conduct 10 trials.

C In the third column of the table, record how many boxes were needed to find a winning code. Circle the trials that required 3 or more boxes.

D Calculate the experimental probability of needing to buy at least 3 boxes of cereal in order to find a winning code.

_____

Trial	Random Numbers	Boxes Bought
1		
2		
3		
4		
5		
6		
7		
8		
9		
10		

REFLECT

1. Combine your results with your classmates and calculate the experimental probability. Do you think this value is a better approximation of the theoretical probability than your result from only 10 trials?

_____

_____

_____

B Based on the theorectical probability, which game(s) has the greatest probability of winning? Which game(s) has the least probability?

Greatest Probability of Winning: _____

Least Probability of Winning: _____

C Travis thinks that lots of people will like Game 5. Predict how many times people will win Game 5 if it is played 100 times. Show your work.

D In Game 5 the prize that is given to each winner costs $0.50. The cost to play the game is $0.75. Based on Travis' prediction, about how much profit will he make if 100 people play Game 5?

E Make a spinner like the one described in Game 5. Spin it 20 times. Complete the table for the frequency of each result.

Result	Frequency
Winner	
Not a Winner	

Find the experimental probability of being a winner in Game 5.

_____

F Now find the profit for Game 5 based on the experimental probability.

G Compare the profits calculated in **D** and part **F** .

_____

_____

2 Drawing a Tree Diagram

Eva's group decides to make gift baskets to be auctioned at the fundraising dinner for the library.

Each gift basket includes one of the items from each group described below:

- A gift card to either Frannie's Department Store or Giorgio's Italian Restaurant
- A bar of fragrant soap, a set of cookie cutters, or a crystal vase
- A watch, a walkie-talkie set, or an MP3 player

A basket of each possible combination of items will be made and auctioned. Bidders will not know which basket they are bidding on.

A Draw a tree diagram in the space below to find all the possible baskets.

B The Escobar family really wants a basket that contains a gift card to Giorgio's and a cookie cutter set. They randomly choose to bid on the third basket that is auctioned, and they win. What is the probability that they win a basket with the items they want? Explain.

_____

_____

_____

3 Using Simulations

Melonie's group sets up a booth in front of a local grocery store to collect donations. Based on previous experience, they know that about 40% of the store's customers will donate money. What is the probability that there will be at least 4 customers in an hour in order to collect a donation?

A The committee wants to develop a simulation to estimate the probability that there must be at least 4 customers in an hour in order to collect a donation in that hour. Design a simulation to model the situation.

_____

_____

_____

_____

_____

B Conduct ten trials and record the results in the table. For each trial use a random number generator on a graphing calculator.

Trial Number (Hour)	Random Numbers	Customers
1		
2		
3		
4		
5		
6		
7		
8		
9		
10		

C Calculate the experimental probability that there must be at least 4 customers in an hour in order to collect a donation. _____

Name _____ Class _____ Date _____

MULTIPLE CHOICE

1. You roll a standard number cube once. Which of the following gives all of the outcomes of the sample space for this experiment?

   A. 1, 2, 3

   B. A, B, C, D

   C. 1, 2, 3, 4, 5, 6

   D. 2, 4, 6, 8, 10

A hat contains 5 red balls, 8 green balls, and 9 yellow balls. Rina chooses one ball at random from the hat. Use this information for 2–5.

2. What is the probability that Rina chooses a green ball?

   F. $\frac{1}{11}$ **H.** $\frac{9}{22}$

   G. $\frac{4}{11}$ **J.** $\frac{5}{11}$

3. What is the probability that Rina chooses a red ball or a green ball?

   A. $\frac{13}{22}$ **C.** $\frac{17}{22}$

   B. $\frac{7}{11}$ **D.** $\frac{40}{22}$

4. What is the probability that Rina does **not** choose a red ball?

   F. $\frac{5}{22}$ **H.** $\frac{13}{22}$

   G. $\frac{4}{11}$ **J.** $\frac{17}{22}$

5. What is the probability that Rina chooses a yellow ball?

   A. $\frac{7}{22}$ **C.** $\frac{13}{22}$

   B. $\frac{9}{22}$ **D.** $\frac{17}{22}$

6. A standard number cube is rolled once. What is the probability that a number less than 3 is rolled?

   F. $\frac{1}{6}$ **H.** $\frac{1}{2}$

   G. $\frac{1}{3}$ **J.** $\frac{2}{3}$

7. A spinner has white, green, violet, indigo, and blue sections. Which of the following is the complement of the event that the spinner lands on violet?

   A. The spinner lands on green.

   B. The spinner lands on white, green, or indigo.

   C. The spinner lands on white, green, indigo, or blue.

   D. The spinner does not land on blue.

8. The probability that a new car at a local dealership has a bad headlight is 0.003. Which statement best describes the probability of this event?

   F. It is likely that a new car at a local dealership has a bad headlight.

   G. It is unlikely that a new car at a local dealership has a bad headlight.

   H. It is neither unlikely nor likely that a new car at a local dealership has a bad headlight.

   J. It is impossible that a new car at a local dealership has a bad headlight.

9. Which event is impossible?

   A. A bowl has 10 red marbles and 12 green marbles. You choose a red marble from the bowl.

   B. A bag has pieces of paper numbered from 1 to 100. You choose a number divisible by 3.

   C. A spinner has sections lettered A through H. The spinner lands on the 10th letter of the alphabet.

   D. You roll two standard number cubes and the sum of the numbers rolled is 12.

10. At A-1 Truck Dealership, a customer can order a red, turquoise, or green truck. The truck can have leather or cloth seats. A customer can also choose a black, tan, or grey interior color. From how many possible trucks can a customer choose?

F. 8 **H.** 27

G. 18 **J.** 36

FREE RESPONSE

11. Yvonne draws a marble from a basket. She records the color and puts the marble back into the basket. The experiment is repeated several times. She records the frequency of each color in the table.

Color	Frequency
Red	7
Yellow	9
Green	14
Purple	10

What is the experimental probability of choosing a green marble?

_____

_____

12. A hockey team has 12 girls and 9 boys. Each week the coach chooses one player at random to play goalie for the next game. What is the probability that the coach chooses a girl to be the goalie for the next game?

_____

_____

The probability of choosing a 6 at random from a standard deck of playing cards is $\frac{1}{13}$. Use this information for 13 and 14.

13. What is the complement of the event of choosing a 6?

_____

_____

14. What is the probability of the complement of the event of choosing a 6?

_____

15. You roll a standard number cube 1,000 times. Predict the number of times you will roll a 2 or a 5.

_____

_____

_____

Use the spinner for 16 and 17. Tell whether each student is correct and explain.

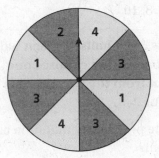

16. Ashley said, "There are four numbers on this spinner. One of these numbers is 2. Therefore, the probability that this spinner lands on 2 is $\frac{1}{4}$."

_____

_____

_____

_____

_____

17. Suzanne said, "There are two colors on this spinner. One of these colors is blue. Therefore, the probability that this spinner lands on blue is $\frac{1}{2}$."

_____

_____

_____

_____

Correlation of *On Core Mathematics Grade 7* to the Common Core State Standards

Ratios and Proportional Relationships	Citations
CC.7.RP.1 Compute unit rates associated with ratios of fractions, including ratios of lengths, areas and other quantities measured in like or different units.	**pp. 35–38, 51–54**
CC.7.RP.2 Recognize and represent proportional relationships between quantities. a. Decide whether two quantities are in a proportional relationship, e.g., by testing for equivalent ratios in a table or graphing on a coordinate plane and observing whether the graph is a straight line through the origin. b. Identify the constant of proportionality (unit rate) in tables, graphs, equations, diagrams, and verbal descriptions of proportional relationships. c. Represent proportional relationships by equations. d. Explain what a point (x, y) on the graph of a proportional relationship means in terms of the situation, with special attention to the points $(0, 0)$ and $(1, r)$ where r is the unit rate.	**pp. 39–42, 43–46, 51–54**
CC.7.RP.3 Use proportional relationships to solve multistep ratio and percent problems.	**pp. 39–42, 43–46, 47–50, 51–54, 63–64, 81–84**

The Number System	Citations
CC.7.NS.1 Apply and extend previous understandings of addition and subtraction to add and subtract rational numbers; represent addition and subtraction on a horizontal or vertical number line diagram. a. Describe situations in which opposite quantities combine to make 0. b. Understand $p + q$ as the number located a distance $|q|$ from p, in the positive or negative direction depending on whether q is positive or negative. Show that a number and its opposite have a sum of 0 (are additive inverses). Interpret sums of rational numbers by describing real-world contexts. c. Understand subtraction of rational numbers as adding the additive inverse, $p - q = p + (-q)$. Show that the distance between two rational numbers on the number line is the absolute value of their difference, and apply this principle in real-world contexts. d. Apply properties of operations as strategies to add and subtract rational numbers.	**pp. 7–9, 11–14, 27–30**
CC.7.NS.2 Apply and extend previous understandings of multiplication and division and of fractions to multiply and divide rational numbers. a. Understand that multiplication is extended from fractions to rational numbers by requiring that operations continue to satisfy the properties of operations, particularly the distributive property, leading to products such as $(-1)(-1) = 1$ and the rules for multiplying signed numbers. Interpret products of rational numbers by describing real-world contexts. b. Understand that integers can be divided, provided that the divisor is not zero, and every quotient of integers (with non-zero divisor) is a rational number. If p and q are integers, then $-(p/q) = (-p)/q = p/(-q)$. Interpret quotients of rational numbers by describing real-world contexts. c. Apply properties of operations as strategies to multiply and divide rational numbers. d. Convert a rational number to a decimal using long division; know that the decimal form of a rational number terminates in 0s or eventually repeats.	**pp. 3–6, 15–18, 19–22, 27–30**

CC.7.NS.3 Solve real-world and mathematical problems involving the four operations with rational numbers	pp. 23–26, 27–30, 35–38
Expressions and Equations	**Citations**
CC.7.EE.1 Apply properties of operations as strategies to add, subtract, factor, and expand linear expressions with rational coefficients.	pp. 59–62, 81–84
CC.7.EE.2 Understand that rewriting an expression in different forms in a problem context can shed light on the problem and how the quantities in it are related.	pp. 63–64, 81–84
CC.7.EE.3 Solve multi-step real-life and mathematical problems posed with positive and negative rational numbers in any form (whole numbers, fractions, and decimals), using tools strategically. Apply properties of operations to calculate with numbers in any form; convert between forms as appropriate; and assess the reasonableness of answers using mental computation and estimation strategies.	pp. 77–80, 81–84
CC.7.EE.4 Use variables to represent quantities in a real-world or mathematical problem, and construct simple equations and inequalities to solve problems by reasoning about the quantities. a. Solve word problems leading to equations of the form $px + q = r$ and $p(x + q) = r$, where p, q, and r are specific rational numbers. Solve equations of these forms fluently. Compare an algebraic solution to an arithmetic solution, identifying the sequence of the operations used in each approach. b. Solve word problems leading to inequalities of the form $px + q > r$ or $px + q < r$, where p, q, and r are specific rational numbers. Graph the solution set of the inequality and interpret it in the context of the problem.	pp. 65–68, 69–72, 73–76, 81–84
Geometry	**Citations**
CC.7.G.1 Solve problems involving scale drawings of geometric figures, including computing actual lengths and areas from a scale drawing and reproducing a scale drawing at a different scale.	pp. 89–92, 103–106
CC.7.G.2 Draw (freehand, with ruler and protractor, and with technology) geometric shapes with given conditions. Focus on constructing triangles from three measures of angles or sides, noticing when the conditions determine a unique triangle, more than one triangle, or no triangle.	pp. 93–96, 103–106
CC.7.G.3 Describe the two-dimensional figures that result from slicing three-dimensional figures, as in plane sections of right rectangular prisms and right rectangular pyramids.	pp. 97–98, 103–106
CC.7.G.4 Know the formulas for the area and circumference of a circle and use them to solve problems; give an informal derivation of the relationship between the circumference and area of a circle.	pp. 111–114, 115–118, 131–134
CC.7.G.5 Use facts about supplementary, complementary, vertical, and adjacent angles in a multi-step problem to write and solve simple equations for an unknown angle in a figure.	pp. 99–102, 103–106
CC.7.G.6 Solve real-world and mathematical problems involving area, volume and surface area of two- and three-dimensional objects composed of triangles, quadrilaterals, polygons, cubes, and right prisms.	pp. 119–122, 123–126, 127–130, 131–134

Statistics and Probability	Citations
CC.7.SP.1 Understand that statistics can be used to gain information about a population by examining a sample of the population; generalizations about a population from a sample are valid only if the sample is representative of that population. Understand that random sampling tends to produce representative samples and support valid inferences.	pp. 139–142, 149–152
CC.7.SP.2 Use data from a random sample to draw inferences about a population with an unknown characteristic of interest. Generate multiple samples (or simulated samples) of the same size to gauge the variation in estimates or predictions.	pp. 139–142, 143–144, 149–152
CC.7.SP.3 Informally assess the degree of visual overlap of two numerical data distributions with similar variabilities, measuring the difference between the centers by expressing it as a multiple of a measure of variability.	pp. 145–148, 149–152
CC.7.SP.4 Use measures of center and measures of variability for numerical data from random samples to draw informal comparative inferences about two populations.	pp. 145–148, 149–152
CC.7.SP.5 Understand that the probability of a chance event is a number between 0 and 1 that expresses the likelihood of the event occurring. Larger numbers indicate greater likelihood. A probability near 0 indicates an unlikely event, a probability around 1/2 indicates an event that is neither unlikely nor likely, and a probability near 1 indicates a likely event.	pp. 157–160, 175–178
CC.7.SP.6 Approximate the probability of a chance event by collecting data on the chance process that produces it and observing its long-run relative frequency, and predict the approximate relative frequency given the probability.	pp. 161–164, 165–168, 175–178
CC.7.SP.7 Develop a probability model and use it to find probabilities of events. Compare probabilities from a model to observed frequencies; if the agreement is not good, explain possible sources of the discrepancy. a. Develop a uniform probability model by assigning equal probability to all outcomes, and use the model to determine probabilities of events. b. Develop a probability model (which may not be uniform) by observing frequencies in data generated from a chance process.	pp. 161–164, 165–168, 175–178
CC.7.SP.8 Find probabilities of compound events using organized lists, tables, tree diagrams, and simulation. a. Understand that, just as with simple events, the probability of a compound event is the fraction of outcomes in the sample space for which the compound event occurs. b. Represent sample spaces for compound events using methods such as organized lists, tables and tree diagrams. For an event described in everyday language (e.g., "rolling double sixes"), identify the outcomes in the sample space which compose the event. c. Design and use a simulation to generate frequencies for compound events.	pp. 169–172, 173–174, 175–178